# WHEN Spirits HOLD MY HAND

## MARGARET BRAZIL

POOLBEG

Published 2009
by Poolbeg Books Ltd
123 Grange Hill, Baldoyle
Dublin 13, Ireland
E-mail: poolbeg@poolbeg.com
www.poolbeg.com

1 3 5 7 9 10 8 6 4 2

A catalogue record for this book is available from the British Library.

ISBN 978-1-84223-394-8

Typeset by Type Design in Sabon 12/16
Printed by
Litografia Rosés, S.A., Spain

WWW.POOLBEG.COM

FOR MY CHILDREN
STEVE, SHAUNA AND GLEN

*Miracles do not happen in contradiction to nature,*
*But only in contradiction to that which*
*is known to us in nature.*
– St Augustine

# CONTENTS

# PREFACE

I saw her immediately in my mind, this missing mother. I saw her small tan handbag, and in it a bus pass, a mass card, and her keys on a little shoe key-ring. I felt her despair and sadness. My skin became very cold. "She's wearing jeans, a short jacket and a scarf. She's showing me her last journey; past a tall building with a large clock. It's in Howth. From the point where she lies, there are clear views of Bray Head and Dalkey."

**+ + +**

I can visualise people and places and things. I don't try to. They just appear in front of me, in the same way as this book is visible to you here, now. I can sit how they sit, move my head the way they do, use their expressions – "See you later, Mrs McGoo."

I had my first psychic experience over 20 years ago. I am clairvoyant, clairaudient and clairsentient. Now I'm 62 years old and spirits use me in every way to convince the people who come to me that they are present, and that they are very real. I'm a "medium" in the real sense of the word in that I act as a go-between for clear and lengthy two-way conversations between the person and the spirit or spirits.

I've a private phone number and I don't tend to give it out. But two decades ago, it started ringing a lot. Every day. People looking for readings. I've never asked anyone how they heard of me. Over time, I came to trust that they were meant to find me. That I can do something for them. That I was meant to see these people who have found me. That I must have something to give them. There are no coincidences.

But I'm not a fortune teller. People shouldn't come to me if they're looking for that. I'm inclined to see each person only the once, unless they really want to come back again. I wish for them to be at peace, to find comfort and then to live their lives, not to become caught up in the dead.

Nor am I a healer. I can't even look after myself most of the time. Rather I'm a channel through which people who have passed on can communicate with and heal their loved ones. I can't heal anybody, but I can facilitate wonderful healing that comes from this higher level.

The spirits call me. I don't call them. Everyone who has come to me has been led here by the spirit world. I don't ask for them to come here and I've never courted any attention. Until now, I've never spoken about what I do. I didn't invite any of these people who come to my door. At the beginning, I was more amazed than they were by what was coming from my mouth. I wasn't sitting down trying to "home in". In fact, I had to teach the spirits manners after a while. It's like having children in the house and needing to teach them their place. I had to learn to control them. There was a time when I didn't want to go out; I'd be getting names and places and messages crowding in on me when I was passing people on the street, but I wouldn't approach anyone. What was I supposed to do with all that information? They can't just butt in, all of the time, into my life. I have to live normally too. Although, if there is something extreme, they will try to get word to the family by appearing and speaking regardless.

I'm writing this book because I've been urged to by the spirit world. It's not for self glory. It's to spread the word of spirit. It's to give them a voice; to let them be heard. When we die, it's another beginning. The soul lives on. And it can communicate its personality, its illness, its name and address – everything about its life on earth. It will comfort a lot of people to know that their loved ones are not just in the ground, a bag of bones. They will see them again.

Nobody can contradict or explain the evidence and proof that's given through me in a private reading. The best readings are usually to those who are sceptical. The spirits go all out to prove their existence – to show off! There will be fireworks! It's good to be sceptical, not to be gullible. I know that with this book I risk ridicule and give those who are that way inclined an opportunity to have a laugh. Plenty have come through my door sceptical, but nobody has ever left unconvinced. Healing goes where it's needed most. I'm not in charge of it and neither are the people who come.

After the early days, as my gift developed and time passed, I became aware that I was advancing through levels within my work. I became conscious of spirits hanging back – "reluctant" spirits, who perhaps committed crimes against others or caused pain in their lives; I realised that I could partake in astral travel; I discovered that I could communicate with Alzheimer's sufferers; and many other "advanced" abilities. I've travelled extensively to help where I can, where I'm called to.

Men and women come from all over the world to see me now. I've no idea how they heard of me and I've no interest in that. I'm only interested in them when they're here. Famous people, ordinary people, people in religious orders. The latter might have lost their way in their own faith or may be questioning themselves. Their readings can ignite the spark in their own spirit. It's all teaching and learning. I learn, I teach; they learn, they teach.

My gift brings me much joy and comfort, but also a lot of stress and sorrow. Families of missing people will contact me to find their loved ones. This usually involves reliving their final moments. I take on the emotions and the pain of the victim, which can be very frightening. I have been hospitalised numerous times in my life with very real – but temporary – illnesses and injuries brought about through my work.

Over the last 20 years, I have seen thousands of people and far greater numbers of spirits. This book is a collection of a small number of the experiences I have had and of my own journey. I have allowed the spirits to speak for themselves.

In the final chapter, *The Necklace*, I include a handful of testimonies – some short, some long – from individuals who have found me and spoken to their loved ones through me. They give their own recollections of these meetings, these healings. All of the stories and testimonies in this book can be verified.

+ + +

There is no secret. None of us are Chosen or are Special. Some of us just develop this gift, maybe through pain or heartache, while others might live their lives busy with other things and untouched by quiet thought or meditation.

Share your knowledge. Whatever God it is you believe in, He does not keep secrets from people who take the time to talk to Him.

Spirits are always just a thought away.

Margaret Brazil
April 2009

# INTRODUCTION

*One evening I was at home and my sister told me a medium was coming over to give readings and make contact with people who had died. I laughed at her and her friend.*

*"You must be all mad! What a load of rubbish. A pack of lies is all you're going to hear."*

*Margaret arrived and the girls got nervous. They brought her straight into the sitting room and left her there.*

*"What's going on?"*

*"She needs to be left in the room to prepare for the readings."*

*I laughed. What a load of bull. I couldn't wait for them to see how foolish they were being. A total scam.*

*My sister was annoyed that I was so dismissive of it*

*all. Being the hard man, as usual. So she told me about her friend – Jackie, a girl I knew well – who had been to Margaret for a reading. We were sitting in the kitchen and I can remember the story so well.*

*Jackie's father had died some time before. He had gone to the Lough & Quay pub with her and her husband. The father started telling them a joke. The joke was about wagon wheels and cowboys. While he was telling the joke, a friend he hadn't seen in over a year came into the pub. He got up out of his seat to greet this friend and fell to the floor. He never got to finish the joke.*

*When Jackie came for a reading, her father said – through Margaret – "To prove that I'm here in this room with you, I'm going to tell you the rest of the joke about the wagon wheels and cowboys." And he did.*

*I was lost for words. I knew Jackie and she was very sound – you know, normal.*

*I thought I'd go in and have a look at Margaret, maybe give it a bash because she was already there.*

*I went into the room. I said hello, and Margaret took my hand. I'll never forget the first words out of her mouth. She said: "Your grandfather – Gembo – is here and he has your daughter Shona with him. She is beautiful, with lovely long hair. He is holding her hand."*

*I was in the room less than a minute.*

*I thought my heart would burst. My baby girl had died, but never in my wildest dreams would I have* thought I could get in touch with her, ever. I never spoke about her. I couldn't. My world crumbled the day she died. She had only lived for a couple of days. I was shaking, trying to hold my emotions back. Margaret said that Shona was telling me to forgive, as I still felt angry and bitter and full of blame over her death.

Margaret told me that Gembo was my guardian angel and, to prove it, he – Gembo – said that my girlfriend and I had just had a row over a key. That had happened that very day. And nobody else had been there or would have known about it. I didn't need any more proof, but Margaret went on.

"He says that you have a lovely little boy now. And there's somebody else coming in; it's Veronica. She's here now, saying hello. But Gembo isn't letting her in! He'll let her say hello, and that's about it!"

Holy shit. It was so much to take in. My mind boggled. Veronica was my grandmother – on my dad's side – and, to be honest, none of us really liked her. She was a tough woman. I wouldn't have been that keen to talk to her at all.

Then she said: "Your mother Betty is from Drimnagh."

True.

"Glen, I see your daughter Shona making her Holy Communion. She's dressed in white and standing with Our Lady."

Had she lived, Shona would have been making her communion a matter of weeks later.

*Margaret told me so much that evening, so many things that nobody in this world but I could have known. I really felt that my heart was going to explode. I went into that room sceptical and came out grey in the face, with tears in my eyes and a lump in my throat. I wasn't able to talk. My sister and her friend looked up, expecting to hear me rubbish it all. I couldn't. I walked straight through the room. My sister started to cry. I left the house. I was stunned. I wandered around the streets crying, but with joy – not grief – for the first time in seven years. I felt relief, happiness; it was better than winning the Lotto.*

*That night changed me and my life forever because I hadn't been coping well. I was having difficulty getting myself out of bed in the morning and I was getting very down. I got everything I needed that night, all those years ago. I don't need to go again; I believe now. I lost my fear of death. I know for certain now that there is life after this world and I will meet Shona and all the others I loved who have passed on. Every single thing that Margaret said was the absolute truth.*

*The next day, I told my mother about the reading. She let me talk and talk and when I finished, she said; "Glen, you've been talking about Shona for the last hour and a half. Do you know that this is the first time you've ever spoken about her?" It was true. Since then, I talk about her all the time. The reading was a great healing for me. I was cleansed, that's the exact word for it. Cleansed.*

*My friend Susan went to Margaret soon after. Like*

*everyone I know who has been to her, she was over the moon with her reading.*

*I recall one thing in particular that Margaret told her, which stayed with her. Susan had been getting her sitting room redecorated. She had a photo of her dad in a frame on a shelf in the corner. Because of the new decor and furniture, Susan had moved his picture to the other side of the room, on top of the mantelpiece. Margaret told her that he didn't like where he was sitting and that he wanted to be put back where he was; that he had a better view of things from where he used to be. He asked – in no uncertain terms – to be put back where he was. He preferred it.*

*Susan went straight home that day and put her dad back where he had been for all that time before.*

*My whole family have had readings with Margaret now and they were all accurate, mind-blowing and comforting. We talk about our readings and are full of gratitude for the wonderful gift that she has. I can never thank her enough. I was in a very bad place and it was the best experience I could have ever wished for. In fact, she probably saved my life.*

Glen Beatley,
Dublin

# ONE

## SERENDIPITY

One night I was sitting alone at home when I saw a movement beside me. On the white wall opposite me an oval photo frame "appeared" and in it a picture of my father – who died in 1969. As true as God. As though I was watching a short film, I could see him walking from the bus stop on the Quays down O'Connell Street wearing his hat and coat and with a newspaper folded under his arm. I watched this for a good five minutes. At least. I kept looking away, looking back. I wasn't seeing things. Now, if someone has an explanation for that, I'd love to hear it. Because I don't.

At this time, I was searching, changing. My physical, mental and spiritual health needed care and nourishment. I was at a very low point in my life due to crisis, serious illness, stress, and the break-up of my marriage. I had always had faith so I decided to let life guide me because nothing I planned seemed to work out anyway. I had so many challenges ahead of me and very little confidence. It was a time of great change. Up until this point, I'd led a very confined life in the house with my three children. I had gone through the years ignoring who I was and not developing as a person, much as many of us do due to our preoccupation with the day-to-day. But sometimes it can be through difficulty, when we actually have nowhere else to turn, that we develop spiritual strength and find our truth.

I had taken up art lessons and taught myself to read music. A meditation group I had joined was helping me to find tranquillity; a spark had been lit inside me. I was questioning things more than before; I was sceptical by nature and tended to be grounded and very no-nonsense. And yet I felt a door was being opened to me, a door I hadn't spotted before, and through it was an unfamiliar world. I didn't know where I was going, but I meditated at home every day and I knew that something was happening, something was changing for me. There was another side of myself coming to the fore. I was being led somewhere.

I met a woman around this time – Michelle – who read tarot cards and was a medium. I was fascinated by the idea that she could communicate with the spirit world. We formed quite a strong friendship over time. She was someone I could share my new life with, my new experiences. Meditation and things of that nature had been alien to me prior to this, so I tended to stay quiet about them around my family, but Michelle could relate to them and help me make sense of them.

I started reading tarot cards by myself. I never intended to use them outside my own home. It was a novel way for me to focus and work things through in my head. I didn't have an interest in predicting the future with these cards; I just enjoyed the focus, the intricate pictures, the quiet time. I started reading them for my children and my friends who might be in the house, but it was only for entertainment. And yet a strange thing started to happen. I don't know that it had anything at all to do with the cards, but I started to see things. To hear messages. My mind became flooded with information for the person smiling in front of me. Private information, profound advice about their personal lives. I was fascinating myself as much as anybody else. Why was my head filling with thoughts and pictures when I sat and concentrated? Was it coming from my subconscious mind, from a mystical place? Was I going mad?

I was being opened up to higher levels of communication. I tried to get a handle on things. I had started to feel peculiar sensations; my hair being stroked, my forehead being kissed. It felt odd and left me looking over my shoulder. I knew I wasn't in any danger, that the very definite presence I could feel beside me, touching me, was a benign one. I was intrigued by it but, at the same time, I did start to leave the landing light on through the night.

With time, I was to learn that this was my own spirit

guide, my teacher. His name is Anthony. Now when I'm sitting in the quiet and feel that very definite stroking of my hair, a hand holding my hand, I love it. I am not alone. None of us are alone.

Months passed. I didn't dwell on the apparition of my father's spirit; nothing like that had happened again so I didn't give it too much thought and I chose not to mention it to anyone. My sister Rita moved into an old house in Blessington with her young daughters. I took a trip down to visit her one morning. While Rita made tea and spoke about her plans for the house, I sat on a bench at the window in the kitchen looking out. So much space to look out upon, so many magnificent strong trees. Beside me, I suddenly noticed an elderly lady sitting as I was, seemingly distracted from Rita's chatter by the view. She'd no interest in me either. Just sitting there, next to me on the bench, looking out the window into the daylight. I was a bit startled, as I hadn't noticed her come in, hadn't introduced myself.

Rita chatted on.

I was thrown by this visitor.

*How did she get in? I was sure the kitchen was empty when I arrived.*

A penny dropped, and I felt the colour drain out of my face.

*She's a spirit.*

I wanted to jump up and run out of the room but I felt like I was stuck to the bench. I didn't take my eyes off her. She was as real as Rita was to me, there, in that kitchen.

"Margaret, are you listening to me? You're miles away." Rita turned to look at me. "Jesus, what's wrong? You look terrible. Are you okay?"

Barely audible, I whispered: "Rita, who's the old woman sitting beside me? Tell me you can see her. Please, say you can see her too?"

"What?! Margaret, stop! You're frightening me. What old lady? There's nobody here. Fuck. Stop it. What's wrong with you?!"

I jumped up and stood next to Rita, wanting to bury my head in her shoulder. She leapt back when she saw me coming. A plate fell to the floor.

"What's going on? Oh God. Please don't tell me the house is haunted. Oh God, no. We've only just bought it. We can't move again. Margaret, stop, please stop."

Rita was getting hysterical, so I stayed quiet and tried to calm myself down. I desperately wanted to get into my car and take off but the way things were going I'd have Rita and the girls with me.

"Is she gone? Maybe you imagined it?"

I sneaked a little peek at the bench.

She was still there. A spirit, but very real. A physical entity; grey wavy hair, soft pale skin. She wore a white blouse, a cardigan and a woolly skirt with flat, laced shoes.

Rita was staring at my face, looking for a clue. Her grip on my arm tightened.

I tried to address her, this lady, with my thoughts.
*Who are you?*
*My name is Margaret. I used to live here.*
I really thought I was losing the plot now. Margaret,

like me. I started to wonder if it was me – if I was being shown a vision of myself as an older woman? I really didn't have a clue.

Three days later, Rita arrived at my house. There was no phone connected in her house yet.

"You won't believe this. Jesus!" She was blessing herself as she spoke. "A neighbour knocked at my door to welcome me to the area and asked if I had seen Granny Nolan yet. She used to live in my house and spent her latter days sitting in the window looking out. Some say they still see her in the window on a fine day. And you won't believe this . . ."

I thought I might believe anything now.

". . . Her name was Margaret."

I was glad. Glad that I wasn't seeing things. Glad that I wasn't going insane.

✛ ✛ ✛

One night in my sitting room soon after I saw the lady in Blessington, Michelle said, "You've a message for me. You've a message from the spirit world."

I laughed like a drain, dismissing her.

"Margaret, you have the ability for spirits to communicate through you. I can see it quite clearly."

"Stop. I do not. I'm going to have a nervous breakdown."

"I've been to mediums in Ireland and England. And nobody has been able to tell me my father's name. I know you'll be able to tell me his name."

"Your father? Is he dead?"

"Yes. You can do it. Go on."

I was sitting there feeling embarrassment and confusion, when I heard a shout – not in my ear, but across my mind, if you can understand that. A clear, loud voice: "WILLIAM, KNOWN AS BILLY."

"Tell me what you can hear. Just say it."

I blurted it out. "William, known as Billy."

"You're the first person to tell me his name. I knew you would." She was smiling.

While I was trying to digest what had just happened, I could suddenly see her father, this Billy. To the right of Michelle, I saw a grey-haired man in a black jacket with black trousers and a white shirt with the buttons open. I could see his vest. His face was very red. He seemed to be trying to catch his breath, holding on to something, trying to breathe.

Michelle saw my gaze.

"Tell me what you're seeing."

I started to. But then my breath left me. I could feel his panic, his struggle to breathe. And then he was gone, the feeling was gone.

"That's my father. He had difficulty with his lungs, with his breathing." Michelle was positively beaming now. "I knew you could do it."

✦ ✦ ✦

A fortnight later, a woman I'd met at the meditation group I had joined phoned me.

"Hello, Margaret, this is Anne. I wonder if you can help me?"

"I will if I can."

"I am due to go to a gathering in a house next Wednesday to read tarot cards, but I'm overbooked. I'll never get through them all. I know that you are quite gifted at this and wondered if you might come along and do some of the guests for me?"

*Pardon?! You cannot be serious. This is a wind-up. You "know"?*

"Of course, I'd pay you."

Anne had rightly taken my silence for reluctance, but wrongly assumed my concern was that I be financially acknowledged. In actual fact, the question of money never entered my head. It was too filled with raw fear and panic.

*You must be joking! I couldn't read tarot cards for strangers. I'd die.*

"I don't think so, Anne. I'm really not qualified . . ."

"Of course you are. Come along and give it a try. I'll be there if there's a problem anyway. But I know you'll be wonderful."

Five minutes of intense persuasion passed before I heard myself agree to be picked up to go to a house in Lucan to read tarot cards. For money. I had taken leave of my senses.

+ + +

I don't recall the details of the intervening week, but I

remember the nervous, sick feeling in the pit of my stomach. I tried to get out of it umpteen times but Anne wouldn't hear of it. She had more confidence in me than I did. She came to my house the evening before and ran through all of the cards and their meanings with me.

I explained to her that any ability I might have was a complete mystery to me. I couldn't be sure that anything would happen for the paying customers that following night. That I just said what I heard in my head and relayed the images that I could see. That I couldn't understand or explain it. And that I wasn't a performer. I didn't know if the spirits would be against my turning up at parties to wow the guests. Maybe that's not how I was supposed to do it? It didn't seem very noble. And I couldn't make it happen at will.

Anne smiled. She would pick me up the following evening at 7 p.m. I hated that, in itself. I like to always have my car with me so I can flee any situation if the need arises. And in this situation, I felt the need might well arise. In accepting the lift, I had deprived myself of that freedom. I would have to sit in a pool of embarrassment and wait for Anne to finish.

+ + +

I didn't speak on the journey to the house in Lucan. My knees were wobbly on the way up to the front door.

The door opened.

And my milkman Charlie – whom I chatted to every morning – was standing there.

I nearly dropped dead.

Our chats had never touched on the fact that I was obviously CRAZY and a COMPLETE CHANCER and that I was thinking of charging his guests for pretending I could read tarot cards and answer their philosophical questions.

I froze. I'd have reversed out the driveway – *had I brought my car.*

*He's going to tell everybody on the road what I do and they're going to burn me at the stake. The parish priest will be down.*

"Margaret! I didn't know you did anything like this!"

He motioned at the sea of expectant faces looking out from the sitting room.

"It's come as news to me too."

I stepped into the hall and pulled him to one side. "Charlie, I've never done this before. My nerves are gone. Anne made me come to help her out. I'm mortified. Christ."

He brought me down to the designated "Tarot Room" at the back of the house. On the way, I caught a glimpse of a neighbour of mine who was there for a reading. I started to hyperventilate.

*Oh Jesus. I'm going to be the talk of the estate. How am I going to get out of here?*

I was a woman on the verge of hysteria. I held on to Charlie's arm. If I could have managed to squeak the words out, I'd have begged him to stay and do the readings for me.

"See how you get on, Margaret. Come and find me if you've had enough."

I nodded and forced out a weak smile.

*I have no bloody car with me!*

+ + +

I lit the candles and set up the cards on the round table. Someone had very thoughtfully left a jug of water and a glass at my side. They must've been expecting me to do a lot of talking.

I sat down and prayed. *Please God. Let me get through this night. Let these people receive good readings and . . .*

There was a knock at the door and before I could muster a voice to answer it, a girl was sitting at the table opposite me, quiet, her face full of expectation.

I looked down. The cards were a complete blur.

*Jesus! I'm going blind with the nerves.*

And then something happened. In my mind I started to hear names and information that seemed to relate to this quiet girl. I started to speak. Blurting it all out. Holding nothing back. Not caring whether it made sense or not. Names of people living, names of those who had died, places she had been, her job, her relationship. Within minutes, I was transformed from a bag of nerves into a relaxed, confident state.

I could see she recognised her life and the people in it. She had a stunned expression.

I was equally stunned. And never so relieved.

+ + +

Over the next three hours, the cards were little more than a prop for me but each of the seven people who came and sat at my Tarot Table left it amazed.

Despite my resisting it every step of the way, that evening was a turning point for me. When I hobbled out through that front door in Lucan nearly four hours after I wobbled in through it, I was exhausted but thankful. Thankful to have got through it and thankful it was all over.

Word about me spread after that. Life on Castle Close would never be the same again.

+ + +

The doorbell rang the following morning.

A neighbour I recognised from around the corner was standing there. I think our children were a similar age.

After exchanging hellos, there was an awkward silence while I waited for her to explain her presence. I thought she was collecting for a charity or maybe trying to sell me something.

"I wonder if I might come in?"

*Pardon? Something must be wrong . . .*

"I heard about you. I wonder if you'd read the cards for me? Sorry to call in unannounced."

And so it happened that word trickled out and more and more neighbours and their daughters and so-and-so's sister and her brother-in-law and so on called at the door.

One night a lady knocked. She was terribly upset. I didn't take out the cards but rather asked her for a piece of her jewellery to hold. It was early days for me and I felt that I needed something tangible to get a handle on the person, something to focus on. When she said she wasn't wearing any I had a bit of a panic and asked her for her runner instead.

She must have thought I was mad. She took her runner off. I put my hand inside it and told her everything that flooded into my head. We got her problem sorted out.

+ + +

At this time, my son Steve was managing a store in the city centre and quite a sizeable amount of money went missing. He came home in a dreadful state. I sat down and took his hand and was instantly transported to the store. I saw a girl – a staff member, by the looks of things – take the money and secrete it in her bra. I described every detail of this girl and of where and when she had taken the money. This put Steve on alert and he caught the girl on camera a couple of weeks later.

I realised that Anthony, my guide, was helping me a lot of the time. He became very familiar to me. I could sense his instruction, "hear" his direction. If I held a person's hand, I could tune in quite quickly.

I never asked someone to remove their footwear for me again.

✚ ✚ ✚

Around this time, a young woman who lived near me passed on. I'd only met Mona a few times but I decided to go to the church out of respect for her and her family. The church was packed to capacity. I slipped in by myself – I'm always alone at these things – and knelt at the very last pew. I was looking up at the altar listening to the priest when a light began to form. I thought it was the evening sun, this beautiful light reflecting onto the altar. But it was an oblong shape. A beautiful, mesmerising light in an oblong shape, maybe a foot wide and long, trailing off at the bottom. The centre of it was thick, the light growing less dense as it widened. It was stunning. I looked behind me. The doors were closed and mourners filled all the available standing room. There was nowhere for a beam to penetrate. It was a curiously specific size and shape. I knelt in the stillness, fascinated with it, gazing on it. It wasn't dazzling or moving, so wasn't from a watch or jewellery.

And then I nearly dropped dead myself.

I saw Mona – the one in the coffin; well, the one who should've been in the coffin – standing in the centre of this oblong light. I couldn't take my eyes away. She was radiant.

There was nobody beside me I knew to nudge or to ask if they could see her.

I sat, staring, my eyes like saucers. My mouth dried out. I could hear my heart beating.

She was there in her full physicality, dressed in a yellow – buttercup, I'd call it – suit. There was a white corsage on the left lapel. Mona stood there for a good few minutes. Her hair glistened and her face was beautiful, happy. And then she faded away, very, very slowly.

I wanted to burst, to ask someone, tell someone, to say it out loud, but I couldn't. What would I say? To whom? I couldn't go up to the grieving family, tell them I had seen their mother on the altar. "It's okay. I've just seen your mam beside the coffin. She looked very well."

I got up and took myself outside. My legs were wobbling.

What good was this information? What good was experiencing this? I didn't know what to do with the knowledge. It was useless to me and yet it seemed so important. Important that I share it, that I make somebody feel better. And yet I couldn't. It would have been very inappropriate.

These were my thoughts at the time. Confusion, mostly. I kept the experience to myself.

When I reflect on it now, I understand that seeing Mona on the altar was part of my being prepared for the work I was going to do, the work that was to come. It wasn't to impart to the grieving family or to share with others. Not to wow or impress people. It was a message for me; I was being prepared. It was part of my gentle introduction.

About three weeks later, I met a neighbour who had been very friendly with Mona. This neighbour told me that Mona had been buried in the suit that she had recently worn to her daughter's wedding. It was yellow with a white flower on the lapel.

+ + +

"Are you the fortune teller?"

"No."

"I thought you were the fortune teller."

"No."

"I must have the wrong address."

"Well, if you find a good one, come back to me with her number because I'd love to go myself."

+ + +

Around this time, my daughter Shauna brought Ariana, a new friend, home with her. While the girls were in the sitting room, I could see a man – he identified himself as Jimmy – beside Ariana.

"Ariana, Jimmy wants me to tell you that he is here. From the spirit world."

Ariana blessed herself. She looked suspiciously over her shoulder.

I smiled. "I don't mean to scare you. He is standing

beside you. He's driving a double-decker bus through Kilmainham."

Ariana's mouth fell open.

"It's my uncle Jimmy. He died when I was a teenager. He was a bus driver."

"Mary is coming in now, 'just for a little chat'." I mimicked her voice, her accent, so that Ariana would know her. "She is showing me rolls of fabric. She was quite a talented seamstress and made clothes for sale."

"That's my grandmother."

Ariana kept glancing to each side, nervously, expecting them to jump up from behind the couch – "Surprise!"

"She is showing me the road sign 'Landen Road'. She is saying it's in Ballyfermot."

"I don't know what that means or where that is."

"Neither do I, but she's very clear on it. Maybe it will make sense to you later."

Mary described her house and remembered holding Ariana's hand walking up the steps to the front door.

"She has brought me inside to the sitting room now. It's to the left as you come into the hall. She's bringing me through the kitchen. The back garden has chickens. There's a man carrying his bike through the house – lifting it and carrying it through the room and down the front steps."

Ariana started clapping and beaming.

"Yes. Yes! That's quite correct. I know that house so well. The chickens . . ."

There were people lining up to come forward. I had difficulty keeping up.

"Who is Helena Reinhardt?"

"That is my great-grandmother!"

"And who is George, connected with her? He's not Irish. Helena is showing me sausages being made in a butcher's shop and the sign – Reinhardts – over the shop."

"Oh my God. This is too much. Yes. My great-grandparents came from Germany and set up a butcher's here in Dublin. George was Helena's brother."

Quite a crowd was gathering now.

"Alice is here. She's your other grandmother. She tells me that you live in her house now although she never met you in this lifetime. She died before you were born. But she knows you."

"Good God!"

Poor Ariana didn't know whether she was coming or going. They were coming in thick and fast to prove themselves to her.

"She likes the new blinds that you have just put up in the house. They are plain – hers were patterned."

"Christ! They only went up on the windows last week!"

"Jimmy wants you to know that he's looking after Maureen, his sister."

The two girls were sitting on the couch with their mouths hanging open.

+ + +

Ariana couldn't wait to get home to fill her family in. She asked her father about Landen Road in Ballyfermot – the address that her grandmother Mary had given her – which had meant nothing to her. He told her that his first job was at that address. He lived at home with his mother when he worked there. The male figure she showed Ariana carrying the bike through the house was him, her father, setting off for work at this job. Landen Road was where he was going to and coming from every day. And yes, Kilmainham was on Uncle Jimmy's bus-driving route.

+ + +

A gentle elderly lady came. She wanted to speak with her husband.

She was very nervous as I held her hand.

"We'll sit quietly and see what happens."

I felt a distinct presence in the room, very quickly.

I could see a clock, showing half past nine, and a male voice saying, "We'll have a cup of tea." I knew he was bringing me back to his final minutes before passing over. I was looking through his eyes. He was watching a match on the television and it was half-time.

I told her everything he showed me.

She nodded, her eyes welling up. This was him.

I felt severe pain in my chest. I knew he'd had a massive heart attack and died that night.

She was terribly upset now. But she wanted me to continue.

Her husband gave me the names of their children, and his two grandchildren; David and Paul. I could see his daughter walking to the Green Isle Hotel and a little child cycling a bike beside her.

He told me that this woman that sobbed in front of me had been invited to America. That their son had gone back to his home there that morning and had asked her to follow him out. She was considering it.

She nodded.

And then I saw a child with this man, in the world of spirit. A child with an angelic glow. I knew this child had passed over a long time ago. I was very gentle. "Your husband wants me to tell you that he has the child that you both lost. He is taking care of this baby boy, your son."

Through her sobs, she said, "Oh, that's wonderful to know! That he is looking after him. It makes it easier that they're together, that they have each other."

"Your husband's parents are with them too." I pressed my hand on her arm. "He wasn't a very demonstrative man. This is what he did to you, pressing your arm, to reassure you."

"That's exactly it. Just like that."

That simple touch reassured her now. As in life.

"I can hear the song 'Tulips from Amsterdam'."

"My other son just came home from Amsterdam and brought magnificent tulips for my daughter. They're in my house. They're beautiful; out of this world."

I stood up suddenly, and said, "Okay, Mrs McGoo, you can go now. See you later, Mrs McGoo."

She laughed, her hand over her mouth. 'Oh my God! That's him. That was a private joke between us. Mrs McGoo! I can't believe it.'

+ + +

I am very close to all of my sisters, one of whom, Olive, runs a B&B in County Clare.

Around this time I went to stay with Olive for a family dinner she was having. I made the mistake of mentioning the people who had been coming to me, the spirits I had been hearing of late. Needless to say there was nearly a riot of excitement. I was sorry I opened my mouth.

"Go into the spare room there at the top of the stairs. It's warm and spotlessly clean. Do a few readings, go on. It'll make the night."

"No. No way. Olive, don't do this to me. I can't. I shouldn't have mentioned it."

"Go on. Just a few. Or one even. Do me. After we've had dinner."

"I'll see."

"That's great." Then she turned to the rest of the table. "Everybody, Margaret's going to do a few readings after dinner."

I could have strangled her.

The dinner – well, the *morsel* that passed my lips – tasted like dry yarn in my mouth. I scanned the familiar faces at the dinner table; family and old friends. Our harshest critics. No way. And I *knew*

21

them; the people in their lives, those who had passed on. Not doing it. No way. I could feel a hot flush coming on.

I took Olive to one side and explained.

"Well, at least do my friend Eva. You *have* to do somebody, and you don't know her. I'll send you up a cup of tea. Go on. It'll be great."

"Christ Almighty! Okay."

I didn't see why I *had* to do somebody. I moodily dragged my heels up the stairs to the room to which I'd been banished. Following me in silence was poor Eva, who bit off more than she could chew when she accepted a casual dinner invitation the previous day. The rest of them relaxed with their drinks, whispering and waiting for a burning bush or some other miracle.

This was to be a great teaching reading for me; the first in which I would learn about pictures and the significance of colour.

Eva had just sat down when a child appeared immediately.

"Mary is here. She is a very young spirit."

"Oh my God. She's my sister. She died as a child." Both of Eva's hands were over her mouth, her eyes wide.

This sister Mary was to be the spokesperson of the reading. She did all of the talking and was a beautiful, gentle soul. She gave Eva the names of their siblings and showed me the house where they lived together; the dining room table with the carved legs where they all sat as a family; the kitchen with the patterned walls.

Eva nodded and confirmed everything.

"Who is Derek? She wants me to say his name to you."

"Derek?! He's my ex-boyfriend. We were very close for a long time but then he ended our relationship. I don't know why she'd be mentioning him. I haven't seen him in quite a while."

"Mary is showing me a picture of him now. Just bear with me, Eva. This is all new to me too. I have to wait for the message."

Eva sat forward on her chair with an expectant look.

The man became an illustration of the human form, as though he was a male body for anatomy students to examine. His body parts – organs, vascular system, bones – were clear. I was studying him, waiting for a message or something I could convey.

And there it was – suddenly, the testicles on this male body turned entirely blue. I didn't know what to say.

*Jesus. Somebody. Give me some clarity on this. This is just going to sound bloody rude . . . I don't even know this woman. She just came out for some Chicken Maryland.*

I put my hand on her knee. "Please just bear with me for a minute. I don't want to give you misinformation."

*Where is Olive with that tea?!*

Eva shifted in her chair.

"I don't mean to make you feel uneasy. I'm not

entirely sure . . . I don't understand it, but then maybe you will." *Deep breath.* "Your sister is showing me a very detailed male body. And the testicles are . . . well, they're blue."

She gasped and her hand covered her mouth.

"Oh Jesus, Mary and Joseph!"

I didn't know whether she was shocked out of recognition or horror. She took a minute before answering.

"Margaret, the man that Mary mentioned told me that he had testicular cancer and that was why he was ending our relationship. He needed time and space to himself. I didn't believe him. I thought it was an elaborate lie to leave me, and yet to have me pity him."

Mary was nodding.

"Yes, your sister is confirming this. He did have cancer. He was being honest with you. She wants me to tell you that this is your healing – you need to leave the memory of your break-up with this man and that part of your life behind. He did not deceive you or leave you for another woman. You need to come to terms with this past so you can heal your future."

That was my first experience of the spirits showing me clear pictures and showing me how cancer looks in their messages for me. I was to see this many, many times from that evening on.

Eva and I chatted on the way back down the stairs, both of us the better for her reading. She didn't share what she had heard with anyone that night, despite the mad guesswork that ensued over drinks – "Are you going to buy that house? Are you getting engaged? You're not pregnant?!"

+ + +

I was convinced now that there was no death of the mind or the soul, just the physical body. I'm not out to prove this, but if I can help someone who is grieving or going through a difficult time, then I will. I am not a fortune teller; I cannot predict the future, nor do I wish to. I simply relay what I see or am told.

Even at this stage, I could see that what I was doing tended to touch on very private and intimate matters. It seemed to be helping people, healing them. And healing, on any level, benefits greatly from the time after being spent alone, allowing it to sink in. My work is not really the kind of thing that great parties are made of. People shouldn't come to me if they want to know what their future spouse looks like or how many children they're going to have. I'm not much of an entertainer.

# TWO

## AN OUTSIDE BROADCAST

It was 1990 now. And the phone was ringing non-stop. Very quickly it got to the point where I had to get a diary to make a note of days and times so there wouldn't be an overlap in my little hallway.

Before each person arrived, I'd be hysterical. Sheer panic. I'd do my best to get on with my day, doing the usual things – loading the washing machine and making lunch – but all the while in a sweat with worry. I didn't know what I was doing and why I was doing it, and I was consumed by the fear of drawing a complete blank when they sat in front of me. What would I say? I'd have to send them away with nothing, having let them come all this way with hope, thinking that I could help them.

But when I sat with them, these men and women

who had travelled to see me, I was quiet and calm. And the words they needed to hear just came to me, or rather through me.

+ + +

A woman with a very strong Dublin accent rang me on one of these early spring days. The connection was very bad so I was shouting.

"Hello? Hello? I can't hear you. Shout your number to me there and I'll call you back."

I pulled over the diary, knowing this was a "work" call.

"I'm in a callbox, love, I can't. I heard that you're great. Meself and a few friends want to have a readin'. Can you come out to where we live?"

"Well, I don't really go to people's houses. Where do you live?"

"Do ya know your way around town, around the northside?"

"No."

As she launches into very detailed directions, I'm worrying about the fact that I have no tax and an unreliable car and I'm a very nervous and inexperienced driver. That's before the worry about what will happen when I actually get there . . . I know that agreeing is not an option, nor something that I even vaguely want to do. To go into an unfamiliar house alone and embarrass myself in front of a group of strangers. Not only that, strangers who have heard that I'm great. The worst kind.

She's still talking.

"Up by Eccles Street, by the Mater Hospital? I'll wait outside the pub across from there."

"How will I know you?" I heard myself say.

"I'm The Blonde."

"I'll pull up outside the pub on Thursday night at about half-seven."

So that was it. I was making a house call. The arrangements were made and I hadn't a clue where I was going or why. Or what would be there waiting for me.

**✚ ✚ ✚**

So Thursday came. And torrential rain fell all day. I got into the car and ran through the route to Eccles Street in my mind. It wasn't quite dark yet, but dusky and very wet. I had my little bag packed with a candle and some music to welcome the spirits. I felt the sweat start to break out and I was still in my driveway. Panic.

*Christ Almighty. What am I doing? Who are these people? Where did she get my number? Why did I agree to go? What if I see a policeman and I've no tax? I'll have to tell him I've been unwell and haven't got around to getting it.* And again: *WHAT AM I DOING?*

The rain got so bad that the wipers were going full blast and I still couldn't see a bloody thing. So I was making my way along, very slowly on the inside lane, passing the Mater Hospital. The pub was at the corner, and it was very hard for me to pull in, so I'd no choice but to mount the footpath. So I'm leaning over trying to see out the passenger window through the sheets of rain. I couldn't see anything. Just faceless figures obscured by umbrellas and hoods, running around my car – probably cursing me – in the rain.

There's no blonde there. That I can see anyway. Good. I'll just get going then. Obviously wasn't meant to be. I feel excitement at the possibility of having been stood up. I hurriedly start debating how I'll turn the car. For a start, how will I even get off the path? Suddenly there's a tap on the window and my heart sinks. I knew the rush of excitement was premature.

I lean over and wind it down.

A soaking wet head appears in it, wearing steamed-up glasses, with other wet heads behind, trying to see in.

"Are you Margaret?"

"Are you The Blonde?"

"I am. I'll get in and show you where to go, but can you give this woman and the kids a lift first?"

Before I can open my mouth, wet buggies with plastic covers are being flung into the back, children in soaking padded anoraks are clambering to get behind the passenger seat, The Blonde has pushed her way in after them and a second woman with a large face has assumed a position in the front.

So we negotiate the pathway and the masses on it, and set off down the road.

With the noise from the kids in the car, and the rain,

and the wipers, I couldn't hear The Blonde's directions. I asked her to sit behind me and speak into my right ear.

Several right and left turns later, we arrived into an area of tall tenement houses. The buggies and the kids and the round-faced woman got out and disappeared into the rain. It was just me and Blondie in the back as I parked under a street lamp. It was quiet. I felt sick. I opened my door, and was met by a throng of people all holding umbrellas. They seemed to have appeared, in an instant, out of the darkness. They were jostling for space, knocking into each other with their huge umbrellas, trying to get a look. I had no idea who any of them were. I could see their expectant faces in the light of the lamp. As though the Lord Himself had arrived in a 1981 Fiesta.

*Oh dear God.*

We all ran to the door of a building – each of them competing to be the one whose umbrella actually saved me from the rain – and I introduced myself. They studied me for unusual or distinguishing characteristics. I think they expected I would look "different". They seemed a bit let down by my normal appearance. They stared. And then a brave one spoke.

"We don' live here. The girl who lives here said we could use her attic. That's why we're here. She's in work, but she'll be home later. We're to go ahead. Up to the attic."

And so we did.

By the time I got to the top of eight flights of stairs,

I thought I'd never regain my breath.

We dried ourselves off and they showed me the set-up, each of them wanting to be involved in showing me around. Like excited, slightly nervous, lovely children. There was a small kitchen/dining area and then a long hallway with a glass door and a bedroom at the end of it. I was to be stationed in the kitchen and they would wait in the bedroom to be called.

There were plates of sandwiches, all for me, and the place was heady with the smell of egg and salad. I don't think they knew what to do with me, what they should say. They had been preparing all day for my coming. I took a few deep breaths. And did some panic praying.

*Dear God. Help me. Get me out of here. I want to go home to bed.*

While I waited for the divine intervention that meant the building would have to be evacuated immediately, I set up the room with the music and candles I had brought. I waited. No fire alarm, no emergency. I was going to have to go through with this.

With all the strength I could muster, I said into the hall, "Who is going to sit with me first?"

Chaos was the reply.

"OH JESUS. Oh fuck. Oh . . . you go first. No, I will. Oh Jesus. No, I can't. Oh Jeeeeeeeeeeesus."

"I WILL! No, fuck. I won't. No."

"You do."

"No! Jesus. Fuck. Okay then. NOOOOOOOOO."

This chaotic banter went on for an age. So I left them in the bedroom to decide among themselves.

They all sat on the bed to smoke and decide. I sat with the sandwiches.

From my chair in the kitchen, I could see them. Ten women on a bed. Smoking. And chewing their nails. Frantic. And then cackling with laughter. Shoving each other. Standing up. Sitting back down. Laughing.

The hallway was filling up with smoke.

The louder ones nominated a quieter girl to go first.

So she came down the hall and sat in front of me. She looked terrified. I tried not to.

"Please don't feel intimidated. You don't have to do this. It isn't a game, but nor is it anything to be worried about. Everything is gentle, you won't be frightened. If I hold your hand, it helps me to connect with your energy and then with the spirits' energy. So I'm going to take your hand, okay? You just relax."

She nodded. She seemed settled enough so I took her hand and closed my eyes briefly to find out who wanted to communicate with her.

I opened my mouth to speak and she pulled her hand away.

"Oh Jeeeeeeesus. Oh God. Oh fuck. Oh wait now, oh hang on. Oh! No. Wait now. Okay. I'm ready. I'm okay. Go on. Sorry."

The hand back in mine.

And then gone again.

Then a deep breath.

"No, go on. I'm ready. Go on. Oh Jesus. No, go on. Oh wait now . . . Go on. Okay. No really. Really this time."

I was laughing now. And then she was ready.

Gently, I gave her the names of her parents, whom I could see standing in the room. As I paused to hear what they wished to say first, she leapt up from the table, opened the glass door and went racing down the hallway, roaring at the others who were sitting on the bed, heads craned out to see – "JEEE-SUS. They're here! Jem's here. Both of them. Jesus. I KNEW THEY'D BE HERE!"

"FUCK off!"

"No way!"

"Oh Jesus, Mary and Holy Saint Joseph!"

They were blessing themselves and sucking on their cigarettes and standing up and sitting down.

The guinea pig herself was jumping up and down. I could have gone home then, so thrilled and convinced was she. It was enough for her. "Oh Jesus. Oh God. Fuck."

I prayed. *I'm never going to get through this night, I'm really not. Dear God, help me to survive this. I don't think my nerves are up to it.* We hadn't even started.

So she came back in and straightened her shirt – the epitome of decorum – and sat back down. But now, in the background, the others were pressed up against the glass door, watching, whispering, listening. The bedroom was too far away for them now. THERE WERE DEAD PEOPLE IN THE ROOM. They weren't going to miss catching a glimpse.

I tried to ignore the comical, distorted faces squashed up against the glass.

I took her hand.

And, in fact, despite the madness of the situation, that girl received wonderful spiritual healing at that first reading. The spirits that came through for her were excellent. No beating around the bush, no coaxing. Just straight in. She had a lot to deal with in her life, and her parents spoke of the difficulties she was experiencing and took her through her journey. By acknowledging her struggle and her perseverance, they gave her hope. She knew they were with her. They took me to the hospital, to the ward her daughter was in. I described it and gave her details of the young girl's condition.

She was speechless by the end. No more screeching or cursing. Calm.

And the others gasping at the door. But quieter now.

Between readings, my car would niggle at the back of my mind. It was parked outside a block of flats with no tax on it. If it was stolen or towed away, it would be a breakfast of triangular sandwiches for me. Kind and warm-hearted as these women were, I didn't fancy spending the night with them in a dark, smoke-filled attic.

So I told them I was worried. From that moment, they took turns going up and down the stairs to check on the car. The word spread around the street that *nobody* was to touch that car. They were taking care of me. They really were. Delighted to be able to help.

+ + +

During the evening, there was a knock at the door of the flat and the neighbours from downstairs came in, wearing their pyjamas.

"Jaysus, what are yis doin' in here? Are yous doin' a séance? Is this one of those séance things? Jaysus, you're after knockin' all the electricity off. The whole buildin's in darkness."

*Christ.*

"What's goin' on? Why is there no lights in the buildin'?"

"Maaaaaaaar-gret! There's no lights in the building. They've blown. The spirits have shut off the power. Jeeeee-sus."

Cigarettes came out so those on the bed could digest this latest turn of events.

"Sometimes the electricity can blow, if there's a lot of spiritual activity. It doesn't happen often but it can. If the frequency is high it can interfere with the surrounding power. It creates a surge and the power can blow. It usually comes back on very quickly."

"NO WAY."

"Fuck."

+ + +

It was very late and there was still no electricity when I gave the last woman back her hand. The candle-lit attic was awash with emotional, hopeful women. All of their children had been mentioned and their hardships eased, at least for a short time. I gathered up my things and set about leaving.

"Are you not goin' to have a sandwich?"

The sandwich mountains hadn't been touched, and now they looked a little worse for wear with their curled edges and the egg contents sliding out at the sides.

"No, I can't eat before or after a reading. I usually wait a little while. But thank you. It was very kind."

They were staring at me. It was clear they were full of questions. I knew getting out the door was going to take a while. So I sat and we chatted.

"I'd love to be able to do tha'. Wha' you do. Jaysus."

"How do you do it? Go on, tell us."

More people arrived into the flat to have a look at me.

"Jaysus. Is tha' her? Jaysus."

+ + +

There were people everywhere. Smoking. I was leaving now. I hugged each of those I had done readings for.

"You were fuckin' brilliant. Thanks."

Some of the others started pushing forward for a hug.

"Missus, give us a hug. I'm her sister-in-law."

As if I was something special – that my hug might have power! So I had to go around and hug all of these people. It was quite hilarious. There I was in a darkened attic, hugging strangers.

They all left me down the stairs, falling on top of each other, each trying to ask one more question –

"Are the angels here? Are they with you?" – putting up umbrellas. They all came right up to the car. Even the neighbours, with their slippers getting wet. Those more in-the-know than others got to stand nearest my door. They were so grateful, and so full of love and so protective of me.

I got the best compliment of my life that night. As I sat into my car, a short girl with big earrings whispered to me as she closed my door, "You're gorgeous."

"Thanks very much."

"Have you got a fella?"

"No, I don't."

"Well, he doesn't know what he's fuckin' missing."

I started up the car and they stood in the teeming rain, with no coats, watching as I drove away, all shouting and pointing me in the direction of the shortest way to get out onto the main street.

I got home and I was tired. But I laughed. They had been so warm and so caring. I was glad that a lot of healing had started in that attic and that each of those women had got what they needed – to feel hope, to move on, to believe in something better than the difficulties they were living. To know that the family members they mourned and missed were still with them through it all. That's the work that I do.

+ + +

The next day there was a phone call at lunchtime. It was the girl who had been pushed forward to go first.

"'Member when all the lights went? Oh Jaysus. Well they didn't come back all night. So we all slept in that room, in the bed together. Nobody would leave. Jaysus, in the dark. And the spirits in the place. But we didn't mind. You were brilliant. Fuck. And all the spirits there for us. Fuckin' brilliant. In anyway, I'm ringing to ask you – do you remember the glass door between the landin' and the room you were in?"

*How could I forget . . .?*

"Well, when we went back up the stairs after you left, we were all talking in the hall and trying to find more candles and then the glass just fell off the door in tiny smithereens! In crumbs! It didn't fall out or in, just straight down in *tiny bits*. Fuck. The screamin' that went on, I needn' tell you! Crumbs of glass everywhere! Wha' *was* that?! Was that the spirits that done tha'? Oh Jay-sus. You've no idea. We were all leppin' and screamin'. We were terrified out of our wits . . . We didn't know wha' to do, so we all got into the bed. Until the morning. The rest of them are still in the room. You've no idea the state we were in."

No lights, smashing glass, cigarette smoke, egg sandwiches and a dozen hysterical women – some of them in pyjamas; I had every idea of the scene. How they didn't set themselves on fire . . .

"It's all right, pet. Calm down. It wasn't the spirits. You don't need to worry. Maybe someone who wasn't familiar with the door just gave it a bang or shut it too forcefully."

"Oh Jaysus. Right. Okay then. I'll tell them all.

That's good. They're still all in the bed in the attic. They're afraid to pass by the door to get out."

+ + +

Around the same time, which was primarily a period of learning for me, the spirits were muscling their way into my life more and more.

A beautiful young girl came to my door one sunny day looking for a reading. She had heard a lot about me. I sat with her and words started spilling out of me.

"Your father is here with an instrument; a lute. He has long dark hair and a beard. He's speaking in Irish."

She nodded and her eyes welled up in an instant. This spirit gave his daughter such wonderful evidence of his being there that she could feel his presence by her side. He told her how he had fallen ill – a stroke – and how he had eventually passed over.

During the reading, a picture appeared in my mind. A photo of Billy Connolly. As clear as day. The comedian Billy Connolly.

*Bloody hell. I'm not telling her that.*

I couldn't bring myself to say it. To say his name. To tell her that I could see BILLY CONNOLLY! I felt ridiculous. So, in my ignorance and arrogance, I started trying to interpret what the picture might mean . . .

"Is your father a comedian?"

"No."

"Has he anything to do with Scotland?"

"No."

"Has he travelled a lot with his work?"

"No."

The sweat was starting to break out on me. I was in an awful state. I wanted to run out of the room. Suddenly nothing I was saying made any sense to the girl. She tilted her head to the side. She was starting to doubt. I wished she'd just leave and I promised myself I'd never do this work again.

I kept going for now. I'd no choice. Moments ago, the girl had been so full of faith. Now she wore a worried expression. She wanted to believe me, but it wasn't looking good. I could feel panic rising inside me.

*What the hell are you showing me Billy Connolly for? What? I don't get it. I don't understand. I can't think of anything else about him.*

But I continued.

"Was he in a second marriage?"

"No."

*Jesus. Shit.*

I wanted to crawl under the couch.

I remembered that when I was being "trained" for this work, my own personal guide, Anthony, instructed me to "Just say what you see". I recalled thinking it was like that TV programme, *Catchphrase* – "Say what you see".

*Okay, I'll tell her. She'll probably walk out, but at this stage we're going nowhere fast anyway. And I'm dying here. Nothing is making sense to her. She thinks I'm a spoofer. Here goes.*

"Look, your father has given me a big, very clear picture of Billy Connolly and he won't let go of it. I'm sorry. I know it's ridiculous. I don't know what to . . ."

"Oh my God! Oh, I can't believe it. That is just amazing. Billy Connolly was his best friend and he flew over for his funeral. He has always kept in close contact with our family. He's one of our longest, greatest friends."

All the time I wasted trying to be clever, trying to interpret, sweating, worrying. Instead of just saying what I was shown. Her poor father must have been exhausted dealing with me! Trying to get the message across, waiting for me to say what he was clearly showing me.

I wasn't happy with myself for causing the girl such doubt for those moments, when her father was doing such an excellent job. But I did learn from this incident and I understood that there is no place for my ego or my interpretation in this work. I am merely the person through which messages, and healing, are given. I need only to be truthful and humble. Maybe that day I wasn't so humble.

Her reading went from strength to strength after that, with very vivid colour and detail. When she left, I went out to the kitchen and made a cup of tea. I was feeling a bit sorry for myself, but immediately the phone rang and it was another person looking for comfort. And so on it went. But in those early days, when I made mistakes, the following reading always seemed more difficult.

+ + +

The next client came and I wasn't feeling too confident. But before I went into the room, I heard the words, "Trust, trust, trust. We do the work. You just listen." It's not easy to do that. To just listen intently and allow yourself to give over exactly what you hear and see – not to "interpret" or deviate at all. When I'm doing a reading, I'm having four conversations – one with the sitter themselves, one with the spirit (and there may be several of them), one with my own spirit guide who is there to help me, and one with myself before I say the words aloud. So it's important that I am completely alert and totally switched off to the outside world for the duration. I must pay full attention and give over exactly what I see and hear.

The girl arrived – Bernie, straight from work and dressed in a suit. She didn't know what to expect.

"I'm not a fortune teller and this isn't for fun, but sometimes it can be amusing and light-hearted, depending on the personality of the spirit that has passed over. You will recognise anyone who arrives for you."

So we waited for a moment – it doesn't take long for the spirits to come through. Often, they will be here waiting in my house before the person arrives.

I could see a young male. He introduced himself to me as her brother.

"Your brother is here."

"Oh God," she whispered.

"It's okay. You don't have to whisper. You just relax."

The next five minutes or so were upsetting for her. In order to give the sitter enough evidence of who they are, the spirit will relate details of their life. I liken it to standing up in court and proving your identity. And often, those details will relate to how they passed on. His was a tragic death.

I apologised to her but explained that this was his way of showing her that she could believe it was him. He gave their parents' names and spoke of mutual friends they had.

The transformation in people over the course of their visit to my house is astonishing. I see them at my door, worried, upset and bereaved; and then, over a short time, the trust builds. It's nothing to do with me really – the trust grows between them and the spirit with whom they are speaking. And this girl was no exception. As we approached the end of the reading, she was relaxed and beaming.

Often at the end of a reading, the spirit will give a present to the sitter; an image for them to take away and hold in their mind. It might be their favourite flowers or a gift that means something to them both. Her brother was standing at the back of the room waving a huge Irish flag. Waving it from side to side. This was the summer of 1990 and Ireland had qualified for the quarter-finals of the World Cup in Italy. *Everybody* was waving Irish flags. There were flags hanging out of windows, stuck to cars, decorating shops . . .

So I'm looking at this guy waving a flag from side to side, and I'm looking at his sister in front of me – her face so full of joy and hope – and . . . I couldn't say it. Or rather, I wouldn't say it. A bloody flag. I forgot, or was reluctant, to just say what I saw.

So, in my mind, I told him there was no way I was giving her an Irish flag as a gift from him. *Get off with yourself. Everybody's waving Irish flags. I need something more for her.*

I needed something else, something more appropriate, something the girl could take away and recall and believe in. So she'd believe in him. And trust in *me*! I was starting to feel a familiar anxiety rising up. *Give me something else,* I pleaded. *Not something so ridiculous that the worst kind of "fortune teller" would wheel out.*

But nothing else came. He was defiant. He continued waving the flag. But now higher and wider.

So eventually: "Listen, I'm sorry, but your brother is waving a huge Irish flag. He wants me to give it to you. I'm really sorry. I know it's a bit obvious at the moment. I wish he'd . . ."

She went pale. Her hand went over her mouth.

"That was his job. He made flags. Often Irish flags."

He was grinning now. Triumphant.

She had tears running down her face. Happy tears.

"I'm so happy. It is him."

When she was gone, I apologised to him. Again. And to my guide, again.

**+ + +**

Word was spreading more widely than I had ever imagined. People were coming from all over the country, calling from places I'd never heard of. I hadn't advertised or discussed my work anywhere, so it really was a very peculiar and wondrous thing.

The calls came thick and fast and the doorbell went; each day people left my home emotional and elated; and still I worried. Now that I was gaining a reputation, there was something to live up to. What if this is the person that nobody comes through for? What will I say? What if they've driven for hours to get here?

As the distance that people travelled to see me grew, so too did my worries. A thought occurred to me; what if I couldn't understand a spirit who came through? What if the sitter was an English-speaking foreigner? Would their parents be able to speak English? Can all spirits speak English?! Maybe they only "speak" in pictures? This makes me laugh now. Spirits can, of course, communicate in any and every way to get their message through. The time had come for me to learn this.

The phone rang. A foreign-sounding lady was *shouting* broken English into my ear: "Can I speak to Mar-gar-ret?" She was ROARING. She had a very strong accent. 'I neeeeeed to speak to Mar-gar-ret. This is Mariiiia. From Colombia. Maaaar-gar-ret? My friend in France, she tell me to call you. I need to get in touch with my husband. Mar-gar-ret, please. My heart is so broken."

I had no idea who she was, who her friend in France might be, how she got my number or what it was she wanted me to do.

"Are you in Dublin, Maria?"

"No. But someday. I live in Colombia, and I need to speak to my husband. *Please* can you help me? I neeeeed you to help me."

I started to panic.

*What am I supposed to do here? Christ Almighty. She was in Colombia! What should I do? She sounded very distressed. She seemed to think I could help. Oh Jesus.*

"I want to help you, pet, but I don't know how I can, unless you're here."

"Can you not tell me on the phone? Pleeease. Where is my husband? Is he okay? I need to speak with him. I miss him soooooo."

*Tell her on the phone? What?! This really has got out of hand. I can't just Dial-A-Spirit.*

I started to feel really frantic. She didn't sound like she was going to be easily put off. Maybe she was a bit mad? Talk to a dead South American man while his wife in Colombia waits on the phone? This is just too much.

"I'm sorry. I really can't help you, pet. I do feel your

grief and I'm sorry. But I just don't know how to help you. I don't think it's possible. If you were here, we could do our best but not over the phone."

As I suspected, she wasn't going to take No for an answer. She was clearly devastated and just raised her voice louder and louder to drown out my apologies, my concerns, my eventual protests.

"Pleeeeeease try. Please try. You must try. I know you can do it. I know. PLEASE, Mar-gar-ret."

And then, I shocked myself by saying into the receiver: "On Tuesday at 2pm, Irish time, you call me again and I'll see what I can do for you, Maria. I can't make you any promises but I will answer the phone and we'll see how we get on."

"Oh, *thank you*. THANK YOU. My life is in your hands. My heart is in your hands. I thank you. I will call. I loooooove you, Mar-gar-ret."

Indeed.

+ + +

There followed four days of sheer panic. I couldn't eat. I barely slept. I couldn't talk to anybody. My mind was too contorted with worry. What will I do? What will I say? *Oh Jesus Christ.* What have I got myself into? What if – by some miracle – Mr Colombia does appear in my kitchen and he doesn't speak English!?

I calmed myself down by preparing a speech of sorts for her when she called. I would tell her I was sorry, but that it wasn't going to work and that I'd be happy to see her any time she was in Dublin. She should keep my phone number and I'd look forward to our eventual meeting. Thank you and good afternoon.

She would be upset, but it was for the best. There was no point in raising her hopes any further. I couldn't summon dead South American men because a (very possibly unhinged) woman was wailing into my phone. Who can?

So that got me through Sunday and Monday. Then Tuesday arrived and I went into another headspin. I was only short of staggering around the house, I was so wracked with anxiety. I panic-bought a long cord for my phone so that I could bring it into my healing room, just in case. Between buying the wrong and then the right cord, sorting myself out with a pen and paper, deciding on the "best" chair in the room, having tried them all like Goldilocks, the obsessive watching of the clock and the trying to actively *calm down* by smoking another box of cigarettes, I had myself in a total flap counting down the minutes, and it wasn't even 1.30 p.m. My blood pressure was through the roof, I had a splitting headache and I was ready to throw up.

Then I heard a man's voice shout right into my ear. "THIS IS BRIAN. I'M MARIA'S HUSBAND.'

*You have got to be joking.*

I started saying the Our Father. *Oh Jesus, Mary and the Holy Family, please help me. This is too much.*

My hair was stuck to my face with perspiration as I waited for Brian to shout again.

"You have to tell her the names Michael and Patrick."

Despite jumping out of my skin for the second time in as many minutes, I started to smile as I wrote the names down.

*Mick and Paddy, is it? Colombians called Mick and Paddy? I don't think so. I'm off the mark here completely. A Carlos or a José, I might believe.* So I told him No: "I'm not saying that."

He ignored me.

"AND MAKE SURE YOU MENTION THAT THEY ARE TWINS."

But of course.

Just then, the phone screeched at me from my lap. I shrieked in response.

The dreaded call.

I picked up the receiver and, confused by Brian's eleventh hour arrival, totally forgot about the pleasantly worded excuse I had prepared earlier.

'Hellooooo, Mar-gar-ret. How are you? I have been so looking forward to today."

"Hi, Maria. Listen, I don't know if this will work at all but we'll give it a try."

I'm looking at the names on the page staring up at me. *Should I say them? Just say what I have heard?* As I'm thinking it through, the words fall out of my mouth.

"Your husband Brian is here. He's a very big man. Describes himself as a big teddy bear, he . . ."

"YES! Yeeeeees, this is him! I always called him my teddy bear!"

"Because you're just a very tiny woman."

"Yes, this is true. I am very short and he very big."

"Maria, why is your husband so adamant that I say the names Patrick and Michael?"

"A high-pitched scream that dogs could surely hear. "THIS ARE MY BOYS! OURS BOYS! Michael and Patrick. Our boys."

"And they are twins."

"YEEEEEESSSS! WONDERFUL. Oh Mar-gar-et. It is really him."

"He is wearing a green t-shirt."

"It was his favourite!"

"He's not Irish, but he would have liked to be."

"Yeeeeeesss. He had a great interest in Ireland. Brian, my love, it is you."

And it went from there. He showed me their apartment in London. He described their boys with exacting detail – their personalities, their interests, their physical appearances, where they lived; they were good boys. He explained how he had died in a small aircraft that crashed as it came into land at a domestic airport in South America. And how she had been waiting for him with her mother when the news came. He had his briefcase on his lap, getting ready for the landing. He was killed instantly. And he loved her to pieces.

And then beside him, I saw a tiny, very glamorous lady with the most magnificent head of soft, white hair. *I am Esther.*

"Esther is standing with him."

"This is my Mama! They are together. I'm soooooo pleased."

In an instant, I'm running along a corridor in a hospital in Colombia and there is a lady . . . I make her out; it is this soft-haired lady, Esther, on a trolley being rushed for treatment. I see that she is applying lipstick.

"That is her! She did that! Oh, Mamaaaa . . ."

The glamorous, tiny lady gave her daughter advice about the family business that she was running with her two sisters. Maria was over the moon. She laughed, she cried. It was perfect.

As the conversation drew to a close, I was ready to weep myself. I was in a state of complete disbelief. I was confused and delighted – for both of us – and exhausted by it all.

"You have given me great comfort. I am soooooo happy. Can I call you again, Mar-gar-et?"

*Oh dear God.*

"And all my friends. And my relatives. They will be calling you. This is wonderful."

*Great.*

I just needed to go to bed.

+ + +

Maria came to Ireland to see me, after many, many phone calls. And today she says that speaking with her husband and mother, knowing they are with her, has saved her life. And neither of them ever spoke English before.

# THREE

## HAPPY BIRTHDAY TO YOU

So the phone was still ringing. Over that past year, there had been no let-up. I decided not to try to make any sense of it. I was learning to be trusting and to just go with it as best I could. And still, every time somebody came to see me I panicked, and I relaxed, and then I learned something else myself, something new.

My very first male client came one dark evening. He was a professional man and I was terribly nervous about meeting him. I felt that a man would be more sceptical of what I "did".

He sat down and I began by backtracking, as usual. Delivering my performance disclaimer.

"The spirits may not come. It is not in my control or of my will. I hope that they do, but I can't make you any promises."

He nodded in reply. He seemed anxious and apprehensive. He kept taking deep breaths, as though steadying himself.

I knew straight away that this man had not been recently bereaved. At this stage in my work, most people who came were struggling with the death of a loved one and came to me to give them strength. I thought that that was what my work was about. Each reading had a lesson for me. I knew this man was not suffering over a death. I went ahead, puzzled as to why he had come.

"Your father has stepped forward to speak to you. He has introduced himself – Matthew, the same name as you. You're known as Matt. And you both share the same profession."

The sweat started to break out on his brow.

"Your father says that you have been a very naughty boy."

Matt looked like he might faint. He took a handkerchief from his pocket and mopped his brow.

I didn't know what he had done and I didn't want to. I was just to say what I could hear, not take away nor add to it.

"Do you want me to continue?"

"Go on. I'm a bit taken aback. But yes. Please."

"You have left your family for a very young lady. He is showing me Christmas decorations and a Christmas tree. You left recently – in December."

He looked at me sheepishly.

I couldn't say anything to console him or otherwise.

It's none of my business. There's no judgement from me. I just give over the information.

"He wants me to speak his words directly to you: What the hell are you doing? In fact, he wants me to shout them at you. So I apologise, but . . . YOU WILL GET TIRED OF YOUR NEW SITUATION VERY SOON. AND THEN WHERE WILL YOU BE? WHY DON'T YOU BLOODY GROW UP?"

Matt was very upset.

"Every word is true. I left . . ."

"Please don't tell me your business. Or feel that you have to explain yourself to me. Your father is expressing himself through me. That is all. He is full of love for you and wants to give you encouragement. He says you've got yourself into a muddle and he is here to help you. To help you find your way out."

His father spoke to him for quite a while. Matt listened intently.

"I'm in a quandary. But I feel that this has answered questions that I have been asking myself for a long time."

"Your father says that this is your choice; he just wants to save you from further hurt down the road."

He sat with his head in his hands.

"I understand. Tell him that I stand chastised and that I'm humbled."

"You don't have to say those things to me, and I'm not here to pass them on. You can talk to him yourself. He can hear you. He can understand your thoughts."

I'm not sure what Matt thought he would hear that

night when he came, and I'm pretty certain he didn't hear what he would have liked. But he will have got what he needed. The spirits are never wrong.

Over the next months, colleagues from his office came to see me on his recommendation. So whether he liked what he heard that night or not, he did believe that his father had spoken to him. My first male believer!

+ + +

A lovely man came to see me a short time later and what unfolded will stay with me forever, it touched me so deeply.

He sat down and immediately I got a strong feeling from his aura; huge compassion emanated from him. I knew straight away that this reading was going to be exceptional.

First in was his mother. She gave her name and their address, which I relayed. I could tell he had an open mind, that he was very comfortable, and that he felt he could trust in me, and in her. He believed that this was her spirit making contact with him.

As the reading progressed, this mother handed her son a rosette and a big trophy, saying to me, "*Can you please tell him 'Congratulations on a job well done'.*"

And then, with the help of my guides and her own guides, she showed me a picture of Mother Teresa. I had learned that when a person lives their life devoted to others – involved in charity work, or similar – I may be shown an image of a Saint or a missionary whom I will easily recognise.

"Your mother is congratulating you on your life's work. She is giving you a prize, but not for one thing in particular, rather for the way in which you serve others with your life."

He nodded.

"Does my mother know what I do?"

"Yes. And she is applauding you for it. I don't know what you do, and I don't want feedback from you or for you to explain things for me; I am simply here to convey your mother's feelings and thoughts to you so that you can be healed and comforted by them on some level. Your mother knows and she is extremely proud."

Again, he nodded. But said nothing.

And then a strange thing happened. A reddish colour filled the entire room where he and I sat. We looked at each other. I felt very cold. I was taken aback myself and looked around the room for an explanation – the sun changing in the window, a red lamp, a reflection . . . but, of course, there was nothing. His mother was trying to communicate something specific to me, but what? You have to remember that it was still early days for me at this work so I was still unsure of many events. I didn't know whether to ask him if he felt cold too. I decided against it.

As I scanned the room for an insight into what the red might mean, a dark hill appeared in front of my eyes. As clear as one would see a hill out a window.

"Just bear with me for a minute; I'm seeing a hill

against this red sky and I'm not sure what it means. And shadows, shapes are beginning to walk over it – outlines of figures, people – they are walking toward you . . ."

This was my first experience of a scene like this, a group of people striding into view, as though they had something to impart. Something important. I mentally pulled myself together to concentrate on them, on what was going to unfold. I didn't want to mess it up for them, to miss what it meant, what was being conveyed to this man. I watched the outlines of these people – more and more of them – coming up over the hill and walking steadily toward this man. Shapes were emerging, growing larger and getting nearer, and I had to focus. I sensed there was going to be an announcement and I felt a bit anxious. I cleared my throat. The figures came close enough that I could make them out. It was a group – mainly comprising men – and at the front a very young male leader; this young man stopped in front of us and announced his name to me, which I said aloud: "Thomas."

"Thomas is leading a group. He has long hair, and a beautiful thin face. He has a pioneering spirit and is speaking for all of these figures that I can see now, as he tried to in this world. He wants me to say his words out loud to you:

"*We were the first AIDS victims to die in Ireland. And we were ill informed. We want to thank you for the great work you have done around this illness in this country. You help many others every day. We are all here to give you thanks.*"

My client was visibly moved and shifted in his chair.

I knew that here in my sitting room was a very special individual, a man with the gift of compassion to see beyond his own needs and wants. And these wonderful spirits had come in their full physicality to give him some acknowledgement.

The room was red, but we were still here. We hadn't been taken away; they had come to us. Or rather, to him. And then they started to turn and leave, this band of people. They walked away, back over the hill, slowly and purposefully, one at a time disappearing over the top. Thomas was the last. He stood at the top and looked back at us and gave a slight wave, before vanishing with the hill.

The whole experience was one of kindness and humanity. I knew in my heart that I would never forget it. And I knew that I would never see the man in front of me again. I've no idea what the experience did for him, but it changed me totally. Even though it wasn't for me, the spirits had taught me something about compassion that day and perhaps removed prejudices and intolerances that I harboured, but didn't know that I had.

The spirits were preparing me for the many people with AIDS and HIV who would come to see me for healing and comfort in their illness and as they neared the time for them to pass over. It was important that I was full of love and understanding and free of fear and ignorance.

+ + +

This experience was only the second time I had seen a large group of spirits together, a room filled with them. Now I see spirits in groups so easily and so much that I tend not to go to shopping centres because often, in a crowd, I can't quickly identify who is actually there in the physical and who is in spirit. I remember vividly the first time I ever saw them in a group. I would say that on that particular night, their willingness to communicate with and through me became very strong. I've never been frightened by them. When I saw them all together that first time, it happened in the safest and most comfortable environment for me. It was a wet Monday evening after a meditation.

Meditation had been my starting point. The only way I can describe the feeling I got from going to my weekly meditation group was that it was as though I had come home. I was always reluctant to come back from this place.

During a meditation, a person is completely free – you are just *you*. You make up your mind to leave all of your worries outside the door – your husband, your wife, your job, your children, your finances, your illness, the lot – so that when you come in, you have cleared yourself of everything, you have stripped yourself and are ready to be welcomed into the warmth of something higher.

When I started, I couldn't wait to get in the door – throw off my shoes and coat, dump my bag and lie down to take in the tranquillity with each breath. One session could sustain me for a week; the feeling of peace and calm. I smiled more easily and worried less. I had been a chronic worrier and slowly I began to let go of this. The changes in me were subtle but very powerful. The lonely feeling left me; I knew there were other realms, that I had a connection with something.

My aura was becoming brighter, looser, stretching out, floating more freely beyond myself. I began to have out-of-body experiences during the meditations but, because I was in this safe place, I didn't get frightened. The first time it happened, I was floating above the group and I could see everybody lying down – including myself. I remember that feeling of complete and utter freedom. I know now that the spirit can leave the human body when you are totally at peace and yet you still remain connected to your reality. I could see a silver chord connecting me to the shell – that ageing body – that was lying, motionless, on the floor. I could move around the room, behind chairs, over the other bodies. Over time, months, I began to see what I now recognise as spirit guides. They explained to me that our bodies are just like overcoats; we take them off when we're finished with them, but we are still ourselves, each of us. Our soul, our mind, our memories. You are still you, living on.

I didn't realise it then, but during all of those early meditations, I was being taught, prepared. I was shown different periods in time, different places, and I learned about various symbols. And now doing my readings with people, when I see these symbols I know immediately what I am being told.

During my meditations, I began to see people who had passed over. Not my grannies and aunties, as you might imagine, but strangers. People I had never met and didn't know, but I knew they were no longer living here. I could feel that they weren't on this plane – these different faces. Some would linger for a while and then move on, some would just pass. I got used to seeing them, as my introduction to this spirit world was so gentle and gradual.

This rainy Monday, I went to my meditation group, as was my habit. I knew the names of all the others in the group, but nothing about their lives nor they about mine. This was a very important and powerful part of it for me. There was privacy and freedom – and yet safety – within this small group. On this particular night, there were just five of us.

Every evening, the experience was different. During this evening's meditation, all I could see were colours and rainbows and music notes, but no people. I recall that it was like watching a huge, Technicolor movie with celestial music. Each musical note seemed to resonate to a colour. I was in the music, in the colours, if that makes any sense. I became the colours and I became the notes and my feelings changed accordingly. I was overcome with excitement and joy, my whole body was tingling. I had never felt so alive. I knew I was learning something important. That I was moving to a higher level. I became engulfed in the swirls of energy. And then the music faded away and the experience started to slow down, and I could hear the quiet music in the room again, the CD – a different music. The colours faded one by one, and I was left surrounded by white. I was learning that different colours and sounds resonate in different parts of you and enliven your body and soul.

It's important after a meditation to bring yourself back into this world's reality from higher levels, into the physical, very gently. I moved my feet, yawned, felt my arms and legs, felt the floor beneath me – became aware of my body, and then opened my eyes. Then it was safe. Safe. I was myself in this world again, myself but different.

Afterwards, I didn't want to talk. I wanted to digest what I had experienced and cherish it, and mull over what it meant to me. I didn't have the words for it. Sometimes the group would chat over tea before setting off for home. We were generous and friendly toward each other, but not intrusive. We expected nothing of each other. We were all soul-searching in our own way, I suppose.

I left the meditation room and smoked out the window in the little kitchen area, thinking to myself, looking out into the darkness, listening to the noise of the rain on the fire escape. Behind me, another lady, Sarah, counted out the cups and put the teapot on the tray. We took turns doing this little job.

"Are you coming for tea, Margaret?" asked Sarah as she left the room.

I put out my cigarette and followed her.

It had only been five minutes since the meditation

ended but when we went back into the room, it was full of people, holding balloons and wearing party hats. I was taken aback. I hadn't heard them arrive. I marvelled at their organisation, their silence. The crowd began to sing "Happy Birthday" at the top of their voices.

*How lovely,* I thought. A surprise party. There were at least twenty of them, singing away – two of them holding a big, round, white, piped birthday cake with candles. They held it up in front of Laura – one of the ladies I knew. I was mortified. I wished I'd known it was her birthday; we all liked to keep to ourselves but I'd have brought a card. Everyone else seemed to be in on it. I joined in with the singing and the clapping, still amazed at how quietly and quickly they had got in and assembled themselves.

So I'm singing and clapping with the rest of them, when the people with the party hats and the balloons start to fade away, fade away, until we are the five again. These other people in their various cardigans, skirts, trousers, some with glasses, some with moustaches – they're gone. Not there. I'm on the "Hip Hip" bit, when I realise I'm doing it alone. And the other four are standing quietly, staring.

Laura, the lady on whom the attention had been focused, told me she was fifty that day. But she had kept it a secret.

+ + +

That was my first time to see a room full of spirits, and yet I didn't know at the time that they were spirits. I wasn't meditating, I wasn't focusing my mind at all. But I could see them, as real as Sarah walking ahead of me with the tray.

The spirit teachers had prepared me slowly and gently before I was allowed to see people from the next world, before they appeared as a group, so that I would not be frightened or apprehensive. Lots of strange things happened to me during that time of opening up.

Up until this, I had survived in a constant winter. The Winter of the Soul is what I like to call that state of always looking outwards, always looking outwards to fill yourself up. Needing the approval of others. Needing to be the perfect wife, daughter, mother, son, husband. Keeping busy to fill the emptiness. The soul becomes annihilated by such outwardness. The soul needs us to look inside, to turn our focus inward, to ourselves. Knowing what you think yourself, of yourself.

The Winter of the Soul is feeling that you have to always be in control, that you have to be the best at everything, in order to ensure that other people perceive you as a success. Those of us who can't be alone, who can't walk into a room without turning on the television for company, who find no joy in themselves. This makes life a struggle. I had lived this way.

But the art classes, music, meditation, welcoming

new people into my home every day – now these things filled my emptiness. When I put all of them together they were the perfect mix for me, for my gift to unfold. I didn't care about the approval of others anymore. When all of these ingredients came together, the cake got baked. And this is the result; this is me.

It was September 1991 when I sang Happy Birthday with a group of people from the spirit world. When I went to sleep that night, I felt whole for the first time in my life.

# FOUR

## UP AND HEALING

I had first been introduced to the idea of healing when I meditated. I learned about the strength of the human mind and our energy. At the start, I saw simply that I could imagine pain and then feel it; that I could ignore pain and it would be gone. Over a period of two years, my guide Anthony spent many hours preparing me as a facilitator for spiritual and Divine healing, teaching me about parts of the physical body and showing me the mental tools I would need to allow healing to flow through me, to reach these damaged limbs and organs. The phone was still ringing, but now some of the callers were specifically requesting healing. I knew the time had come for me to put what I had been learning into practice; that, somehow, I was going to be able to help these people.

An older lady told me she was in a bad way and needed healing. That was all I knew. I don't know anyone's business, I don't know what has brought them to me, and I don't pry into their lives. I don't know which part of their physical or emotional body a person is seeking to repair or restore. It's not important for me to know that. I am not a doctor and I don't home in on one area. I have no prior knowledge of the person or their complaints. I am guided by the spirits and I just go with it. What is important to me is that the person does not feel vulnerable or anxious. I always put a light blanket over them as they feel less exposed lying there if they are physically covered.

She took off her coat, hat and shoes and I helped her up onto the plinth in my front room. I covered her over. I explained that I would open her up on various levels and ask the spirits to come to heal her.

"At a certain point, I will be told that it is time for me to leave the room and for your healing to take place. I can't stay in the room because I can't take your healing. I will put the music on low and I will cover you in a blanket. You are safe and you can relax."

I asked Jesus to bring her spirits to her, so she could receive the healing she needed, whether it be emotional, physical or mental. Within a few seconds, I could see a figure clearly – an elderly lady standing at my client's head.

"Who are you?"

*My name is Kathleen.*

"Joan, do you know a lady called Kathleen?"

She opened her eyes. Wide.

"Yes, she is my grandmother."

I felt then that more than one spirit was present. With great reverence I concentrated as other figures began to take shape in my front room. As their form became clear, I got a bit of a fright.

Five nuns surrounded Joan.

My mind started racing, questioning where this was going, if anywhere.

*Jesus. What's going on . . . ? What are they doing here? This woman just came for healing. Why are they staring at her? Bloody hell. I'm not sure about this . . . Maybe I'm wrong. But those are definitely habits and veils.*

I felt on shaky ground, to say the least. It was quite an intimidating situation, if I'm honest. And I knew it might sound more than a bit far-fetched, possibly a bit spooky even, when I said it out loud, very cautiously: "There are five ladies here, with Kathleen. They are standing very close to you, gazing upon you. The five of them actually appear to be nuns?"

Tears ran down her face.

"Kathleen, my grandmother, her five daughters were nuns. I can't believe they're here."

*Neither can I.*

"Joan, we have moved into the spirit world on the way to the higher place where healing comes from. Your family have come to see you and bring you love, but they cannot go on your journey with you. And they cannot heal you. You will receive your healing at a higher level than the place where they are and then you will come back to your own path here on earth."

I was listening to myself speak, making sense of this for myself as much as for her. The words were tumbling from my mouth, explaining, comforting, coming through me but from somewhere else.

"Your elders have just come to say hello and wish you well on your journey. It's just the same as if you were taking a trip here on earth and passed through a place where your relatives lived. You might stop and visit, but it would not be your final destination. They would be there to wish you well, knowing you were passing through and not staying this time, and then you would move on."

All of this made sense to me, although it was my first experience of this nature. It was at once utterly simple and totally profound. It was an experience of great learning and prepared me a little more for all that was to come.

The nuns faded away then as they must, and Joan's spirit went up through all of the levels to receive her healing. When I re-entered the room some time later, I brought her back down through the levels to this realm and closed her down. This is very important – that a person's energy and field is not left exposed and open after spiritual healing. It's like stitching up a wound.

To me, spiritual healing is the most sacred, tranquil experience a person can have. Money couldn't buy what it gives. But the outcome of the person's healing has nothing to do with me. I have learned to let go of the outcome. I am the channel for the spirits. Whether they come for a healing session or for a reading, the people who come will experience powerful healing. I don't have any need for people to phone me back to let me know how they got on, to check in with me – unless of course they wish to. The spirits are the only healers. It is they who do the work, they who convey the messages.

**+ + +**

One evening, a girl arrived for a reading at her appointed time, with two other girls in tow. And they were giddy. Giddy on the doorstep, giddier in the hall. I took it to be nerves.

I had learned from my experience with the girls in the attic so I plunged straight in and tried to grab control of the situation.

"Who's going to go first now?"

There was a bit of nervous giggling and hopping about, and one stepped forward. I ushered her into the room and shut the door before she had a chance to rethink things.

She sat down in the room.

Before a reading, I have emptied myself of my own thoughts and worries and I also do my best to leave any ego outside the door. I am merely a vehicle.

"I wish you well in your reading and I hope that you get the healing that you are looking for."

*Giggle.* "One of my friends is very nervous."

"You are here for you. Don't worry about anyone else. This is your reading, so I'm going to sit beside you and hold your hand for a moment. We'll just sit quietly for a bit and see what happens. I will tell you exactly what I feel, what I hear, what I see; I can't add to it, and I can't take from it."

"Oh. Right. Okay."

I never know what to expect from a reading; each one is completely different and the messages mean nothing to me but everything to the sitter. Each spirit has their own way of communicating; they are individuals, just as living people are. Some are very shy, some are very articulate, but they all do their very best to give enough evidence so their loved one recognises them and knows that they are still part of this life and that they live on, albeit on a different level.

Her father Patrick – *"but I'm known as Pat"* – introduced himself almost immediately.

"Oh my God. Is he really here?"

"Yes, he's really here. And he has no problem talking to you – a lot of male spirits are not very talkative, but your father is. In fact, he can't get the words out quick enough for you."

*Smile.* "He was always a yapper. Never stopped talking."

Pat gave this woman great evidence of his identity – he described the house that they lived in, and how she had come back to live there with him as an adult, and all about her own life. He was amusing and full of fun.

His daughter began to cry. But she was still smiling.

"Oh Jesus! What a sight! Carol, I have to say what I see, and I can clearly see your dad. He's here parading around in a pair of long johns and a vest, laughing to himself, and it would be fair to say he's not in the best shape in the world . . . !"

The three of us were laughing now.

"That's exactly how he went about the house! You don't have to say another word – I know it's him."

"Well, he's not finished. He's straightening himself up here . . . Revving up for something . . . Would he be about to sing?"

"I don't believe it . . ."

Pat stood up straight in his underwear, chest out, head aloft, eyes closed, and with that I began to bellow:

*"So deeeeep is the night*
*Nooooo mooooon tonight*
*Noooo friendly staaaar*
*to guide me with its liiiiiiight . . ."*

And I kept going until he finished the whole bloody song. If he had given me time to draw a breath, I'd have begged him to stop. A good five minutes of revving and bawling and howling "So Deep is the Night".

When the laughter died down and his performance was over, he sat quietly and still. He became calm and serious and now I could just see his face. He was wearing a very loving expression. I watched – it makes me cry even now as I recall it – I watched as he gently kissed his daughter on the head. I was going to say it, to tell her what he was doing, but I held back. I was inwardly debating the fact that mentioning it might put

73

the thought into her mind, when she put her hand up to her head.

I smiled. *Well done, Pat.*

"I feel as if my hair has been moved . . . ?"

"That is where your dad kissed you on the head. I watched him do it, just now, but I wanted you to experience it and to feel it for yourself."

"He was such a character. And he was taken so young. I can never get over his loss."

"You may not get over the loss, but you will accept it, you will get through it. And when you feel your hair being moved, know that he is there."

"Do I have to come back to you to talk to him?"

"No. You can talk to him, anytime, by yourself. With your mind. Everything is mind to mind in the next level. You can light a candle for him or play his music, if you wish. He will know it is for him."

"Where is he going now?"

"He's going home with you. He's certainly not staying here with me!"

**✝ ✝ ✝**

A small, grey-haired lady in a tidy woollen coat and brown lace-up shoes knocked at the door and asked me if I read the tea leaves.

"No, I can't do anything like that. I can't tell your fortune. I tune into people who have passed over, your loved ones, people belonging to you."

She looked a little confused.

"Oh. Right. I'm sorry, I thought you did the tea leaves."
Pause.

"Okay, then. Would you mind 'tuning in' for me? Seeing as I'm here. If you don't mind?"

"Are you sure?"

"Yes. Sure, go on. Please."

The first person who came through for this lady, Josie, was an old boyfriend; I felt we might have been going back about sixty years. He threw flower petals all over her because he could see she'd had a very big celebration recently.

She nodded, clutching the top of her handbag and looking stunned. She told me she had just had a surprise party for her eightieth birthday.

And then, as though a bus had just pulled up, her mother, father, three brothers and a young niece – who had recently passed over as the result of a brain tumour – came through all at once. Each identified themselves by name, rank and serial number. They reminisced with her about their time here together.

Her mother Helen stayed for a long time and talked about the shops Josie had been in that past week, the things she had bought, the things she admired but didn't like to spend on.

"You are going on a trip this weekend, which was a gift for you for your birthday, and I'll be with you," she told her.

Afterwards, Josie was calm and happy, but still a little stunned and overwhelmed. She sat for a while and my son Glen made her a pot of tea – bags, no leaves.

# FIVE

## LIFE PLANS ME

There is a "For Sale" sign lying on the ground at the side of my house as I write this. Technically, my house is for sale. But I haven't had the time to get myself organised, to get the house organised, to even stand the sign back upright since it blew over in the wind two years ago. But I don't worry about such trifles any more. My house will sell, if it is to sell. Sign or no sign. I was very different twenty years ago. That sign wouldn't have lain a single night on its side.

I no longer make plans in my life, for my life. Since those first spirits muscled their way into my days and knocked my own plans on the head. As they found me, and their loved ones came to find them, my time has been out of my hands. I don't control what happens to me and I have come to realise that very little is on my terms. But by abandoning my plans, I have found my path.

In the early days, the lack of control unsettled me. I raged against it. It was difficult to accept that the phone was ringing and people would come whether I wished it or not. As my gift developed, and time passed, it became clear that in many ways I am a passenger. I would feel a presence in the house and the doorbell would ring, and what I wanted to do that day, that week, was immediately relegated to second place.

I perceived it as intrusion in those early months. I see now that, far from intruding into my life, these people, these spirits, are my life. I am happier than I have ever been before.

Because the children were grown up now, I was often alone at night in my house. I often saw lights dancing in the room, sparkling on the ceiling in the darkness. I was never frightened – I was introduced to different levels in such a gradual way that I never felt anxious or worried.

I had come a long way; I no longer had qualms about telling a sitter exactly what I saw and what I felt, without fear of ridicule or of being wrong. More often now, the words would not be my own. I would use the vernacular and the tone of the spirit who was present. They would give me their voice, their expressions, their gestures. My confidence had grown over the years and now I was more relaxed. The people kept coming, and I kept sitting with them. No two readings were ever the same.

I had my first experience of overshadowing around this time. It was a completely new and unheard-of experience for me. Overshadowing is when a spirit impresses their body, their thoughts, their mind onto a living person; our energies merge. The spirit person uses all of me to portray their feelings, their habits and actions. The client can see for themselves the changes in me; perhaps in the size of my hands, that my ankles become swollen, that I take on the exact cough that the spirit had; it won't be my cough, it won't be my expression.

Sometimes I will sit exactly the way the spirit sat, rub my forehead or scratch my head. I may stand up and get out of the chair and walk; all my movements replicating theirs. I might carry their distinct and recognisable smell; a certain perfume or hand lotion, maybe alcohol. All of these factors facilitate instant recognition for the client in identifying the person who has passed on. When the overshadowing is over, I am protected and nothing of the spirit remains with me.

The readings were at a more advanced level now; I would ask the sitter to watch me, as it would be quite common for my actions to be significant to them, as they were not my own but rather the very recognisable actions and movements of their loved one. They would impress their idiosyncrasies "onto" me; I might throw my head back, twirl my hair, cough in a certain way, slap my leg, all the while using very specific expressions – "Catch you later, Horse." I might walk – with their gait – around the room whistling a certain tune, maybe giving a little hop every so often.

It was wonderful for the person in front of me to witness this, to witness the antics of their husband, wife, mother or father; things they might have lived without for some time.

Sometimes, the spirit would overshadow my body and take me to the time of their passing. I would take on their movements, their words, the way they lay in the moments up to their death. My arm would sit in a certain way if they had an intravenous drip in it. My hand or my leg might swell or become bruised for the duration of the reading, as it had been for the now deceased person. I was astonished by this myself when it first happened but I wasn't unsettled. And although it could sometimes be upsetting for the person to recall these moments, such a visible and physical manifestation of their passing also brought immense healing and confirmation of their continued existence in another world.

I was very comfortable with my work now and thought that nothing would shock me again.

And then Denis arrived.

+ + +

Denis had booked a healing session for one winter evening. As always, I didn't ask him why he was here, what he was seeking. He lay up on the plinth and I covered him over. I opened up his centres to receive the healing he needed. When the time comes and I know the healing is about to take place, I remove myself from the room and wait outside the door. The spirits will let me know when I'm to go back in.

This evening, when I opened the door in my hallway to go back in to Denis, I immediately noticed the candle-lit room was significantly brighter than when I had left it some twenty-five minutes before. It was a very dark evening, so the light was not coming in through the window.

I immediately went to the head of the plinth to see how Denis was doing.

*Jesus Christ!*

My breath left me. I didn't know whether to call someone – there was nobody else in the house – or run out into the street.

You will have to excuse me for this – it sounds more than a bit mad – but Sean Connery now lay where Denis had been. And Sean wasn't looking his best at that. Without putting too fine a point on it, it looked like the corpse of Sean Connery.

I looked away, and looked again.

I went around the other side, for a different perspective.

And still a waxy Sean Connery lay in front of me.

*What in God's name . . . ?! Where is Denis gone? Oh Christ Almighty! WHAT HAVE YOU DONE WITH DENIS?*

When I recall it now, it makes me laugh but it was absolutely NOT FUNNY at all at the time.

As I stood, panicking and sweating, Denis' face started to reappear and within minutes there was no trace of a dead James Bond in my sitting room.

*Thanks be to God.*

I pulled myself together and brought Denis round gently and closed him down. After some time he sat up and had a glass of water. We spoke about his healing and he was quite overcome with happiness.

I hadn't said a word about the "incident" at the end. I couldn't bring myself to. I didn't want to frighten him with talk of the corpse of a (living) actor . . . And more honestly, it was quite likely that this would confirm my standing as a total nutcase. I could do without the rumours.

But after a few moments and against all good sense, honesty got the better of me.

"Listen, Denis; when I came back into the room –"

"Did you leave the room? I didn't hear you."

"Yes, I did. And when I came back in, the room was very brightly lit. But when I looked at you, it was, well . . . it was Sean Connery lying on the plinth. His hair, his face, everything about him . . . Sorry, I know this is a bit hard to believe."

"What?!"

"Yes, I'm sorry. But you had vanished completely. Or rather you had been 'overshadowed' by Sean Connery."

I knew I was making no sense and I spoke faster, trying to explain the inexplicable.

"I know that Sean Connery is living, so it isn't logical at all but this is what happened. I don't mean to frighten you. I don't know what this means. I got a bit of a start myself, I have to say . . . But definitely, it was as though Sean Connery – well, a dead Sean Connery – was lying there."

I bit my lip. And waited for a reaction.

Silence. And then: "Margaret, this is the best evidence that you could have given me."

"Pardon?!"

"My father was the absolute image of Sean Connery. Everybody said it. He was like his double. He could have worked as his lookalike. He is deceased."

*Holy Mother of God.*

I can't explain how his father had superimposed himself on his son for me to see. That was my first real experience of witnessing an overshadowing. And this is my first time to tell this story.

+ + +

A woman in her forties came to see me. Her name was Anne and she had the most beautiful soft face, gorgeous long hair. But a look of profound sadness in her blue eyes. I felt I should be extra-gentle with this lady. She looked fragile, delicate.

She sat down and started to cry before saying a word.

I put my hand on hers. I had no idea why she was here or what her pain was.

"I promise to tell you everything that I see, hear and feel. I wish you the best."

The next hour or so was to be another first for me. Immediately her mother stood beside her.

"Your mother is here. Her name was Margaret, but most people knew her as Gretta. She is a very elegant, beautifully dressed woman. She is directing me to look at – oh! It's the most adorable, blond little boy standing at her legs. A young boy – your son."

She sobbed loudly.

My heart broke for her – this gentle woman who had lost her little boy.

"This is why I'm here."

Suddenly, I wasn't in the room. I was elsewhere, outside. In an instant. I was under a car – I've never been under a car in my life – and it was all black to one side, the carriage of the car, while from the other side I could see the sky and a woman's legs wearing tights and shoes. It wasn't me under the car. I could see out, but my head was right under the car. The smell of petrol. Everything was vivid. It was a bright clear day.

My heart was thumping. This had never happened to me before.

Now I was myself, but at the scene. The little boy smiled up at me from under the car.

*Oh my God.*

I was back in the room. In the silence. This heartbroken mother in front of me. Patiently waiting for me to speak, holding a hanky to her nose.

Did her darling boy do this to me, so that I could comfort his mother? Or was it Anne's mother, to give her daughter belief and consolation? Or something else. I can't explain it.

I relayed to Anne what I had experienced.

"That's it exactly. He just dashed out, and before I could grab him he was under the wheels of a car."

She was crying into her hands.

"I watched it happen. I couldn't do anything."

I felt a bit all-over-the-place but didn't say that I had never experienced this before. Bereaved people don't want to hear about my shock.

"Your son felt no pain. I lay, as he lay, and he felt nothing. It was over immediately. Calm."

"Yes, he died at the scene."

"He is smiling now. His soul is happy."

Little Ben – he gave me his name – called his address out to me.

I relayed it to his mum.

Her eyes were wide with joy, joy through the pain. She knew it was him. No doubt.

+ + +

I was broken-hearted for her when she left. I thought about it that evening and I think Ben must have been the spirit to bring me to the place of his death. To make me be him, for a moment. To smell the smells, to see the sights as he passed over, to be him. Nobody else could have experienced what he could see and smell, or could have shown me that he felt no pain, that he was gone from this life in a moment.

I felt very privileged that a spirit would trust me to this extent. That I could help his mother by describing his experience on that life-changing day. I don't pretend that I can make people feel better, that a bereaved mother will come to me and leave with a happy heart, but the spirits do bring much comfort to those who need it. Anne knew when she left that her son was with his grandmother in the next life and that his soul is with her always. She knew he felt no pain as he left this world that day, and that she would see him again.

That experience is as vivid in my mind today as it was ten years ago, and it was to be the first of many of a similar nature.

+ + +

Paul was a businessman. He sat in front of me, while his wife waited in my kitchen. Although I was looking at him on my couch, arms folded, suit on, I could "see" him with his shirt sleeve rolled up and his blood pressure being taken.

"Sorry, Paul, I know I haven't even greeted you yet but I can see you having your blood pressure taken."

"I've just come from the doctor's! Ten minutes ago I had my blood pressure taken. Did you know? My wife must've told you!"

I laughed.

"No, I didn't know. I don't know anything about you."

"Ah, come on. You're making me nervous now."

"Well, William is here to put you at your ease. Your father. He's standing next to you."

"Where? Here!? My dad?"

He sounded shocked. As though he'd come to the wrong place. As though he'd popped in to pick up the paper and some bread and got a medium instead.

I smiled.

"Yes, here."

He looked around, bewildered.

Suddenly, I was gone. My physical body sat motionless in the room, but the rest of me was somewhere else.

It's a cold, dark morning and I'm sitting on a horse-drawn cart. There are milk-bottles rattling behind me. And I'm smoking. I can see a few lights scattered here and there; the odd light in a house, street lamps few and far between, but pitch black otherwise. I'm a milkman. I'm on my way home. I'm blowing on my hands and rubbing them together to keep them warm. Sucking on a cigarette.

And then I'm Margaret again – myself. Back in the room, looking at Paul, who is still looking around, perplexed.

I told him where I had been.

"Go 'way! That's my father. He was a milkman. God. I used to go the odd time with him, on the cart. Those freezing mornings."

"He's telling me where he's buried and that there's land nearby that's very important to you, to the family."

"Good God! That's unbelievable. There is too!"

Paul's father spoke to him at length; about his

family, his marriage, his work. Before he left, he asked me to let his son know he was with him every day.

"William wants you to know that he sits in your glass conservatory where the blue furniture is."

The colour drained out of Paul's face.

"We have just done the conservatory up and the chairs are blue."

"He says it's probably the only place in the house he'd be allowed smoke."

Paul laughed and shook his head. He was more comfortable now.

Although I probably made him wary of sitting on those new blue chairs.

# SIX

## FREE TRAVEL

I had a lot to take in, to adjust to; I was still very much a pupil and the spirits were teaching me new things all the time. Just as I would reach a comfortable level, a secure plateau of understanding, something new would be shown to me. Although at times I was overwhelmed, I embraced all I was taught. I mulled things over and trusted completely. Any doubts I may have had had long since left me.

I knew that everything I was doing came under the one umbrella of healing. I don't mean to suggest that I considered myself a healer, but rather that healing energy was coming through me. I was "plugging into" another system, and it was running through me. Like electricity, power – we know it's there even though we cannot see it, because we see and feel its effects.

There is a power beyond this realm that knows where healing is needed most. I am always, always in awe of the way that spirits work through me. Astral travel – bilocation as it is known – is one such way. This is the process by which a person can be in two places at once. The physical body may be in the kitchen in Dublin making tea, whilst simultaneously experiencing the reality of somewhere else at that very moment; seeing the people there, smelling the smells, feeling the sun or the rain, experiencing the reality of that exact time.

+ + +

One afternoon after I had done a number of readings, I sat down in my sitting room with a cup of tea. And then I left my body.

This was a first for me.

I was in Jerusalem. I don't know how I knew this – I'd never been there, but I knew. I can remember the colours in the sky, the warm breeze. I was standing on a ladder, which struck fear in my soul as I'm afraid of heights. I could feel the wood under my hands as I climbed this ladder. I was there, in every sense of my being. And then, I was staring at a young man on a cross. Immediately, my silly fears left me. I could see his face, his teeth, the wounds. His eyes looking back at me. I felt a flood of emotion; pain, sorrow, compassion. My heart was wrenched from my chest. I wanted to take this young man in my arms and bring him home.

I was there. Nobody can tell me that I wasn't. I will never forget a second of the experience.

The top of the ladder was leaning against the cross. My total shock was only exceeded by my utter humility and privilege.

When I felt myself back in my sitting room, two hours had elapsed. The tea was cold beside me and the room was dark. I heard the key in the door; my son Glen arriving home from work. The kitchen was quiet and there was no dinner waiting.

This was a first for him.

I didn't say where I had been. I never asked for an experience like that. Never expected it. I had been sitting down to watch *Countdown*.

This was the beginning of what I now know to be astral travel, or what I like to call free travel. I have been to far-flung places, and it costs me nothing but energy. As I turned it over in my mind that evening, I couldn't see then how this was going to be of use to me in my work. And yet I knew that was its purpose. It wasn't a gift just for me.

+ + +

Days later, the house was quiet as I sat in my front room reading. And without any thought or effort from me, I suddenly found myself on top of a very high mountain. I looked around me at the mountains in the range and the gorges; everything seemed to be different vivid shades of purple and breathtakingly beautiful. I was sitting, alone, on this mountain. I looked about to get my bearings and take in the colours, the beauty, not caring where it was or why I was there. I was there in every sense of the word; my physical self, my mind, all of me.

To the left was a narrow pathway, where grass was worn away from footfall. I saw a huge man approaching. He had a kind, rounded face and a white beard and moustache. I wasn't afraid; rather, I was mesmerised by him. I could see he was carrying something. I went to move but he put his hand out: "Stay where you are, little one." (This was the only time I've been referred to as "little" in my life! I thought it was rather kind of him.) I didn't move. He sat down. I wondered if he lived nearby.

He handed me a pencil. I took it.

"I want to introduce myself to you. My name is Simon."

This sounds utterly crazy, but it's the truth.

"You know you have to write a book."

"I'm trying."

"I'm here to help you. Write down what I give you."

Now I was starting to wonder just what was going on and why he was here.

"You have to write it. It is needed for the masses."

Now I was getting a little uneasy. I don't think the "masses" will be reading anything I write, I thought. I decided just to listen to him, to hear him out, and politely be on my way.

"I'm here to help. You need to talk about yourself;

the flower wilting, your soul asleep all winter. The soul is the Sleeping Beauty."

He went on for some time about the soul awaking to its potential, to spring, to life, and explained what he meant. It made sense to me. I have these dated notes here, the notes I wrote with his pencil that day on the purple mountain.

"Gently does it. Don't rush. These are unchartered waters for you and I will be your compass. I must lower my energies, my vibrations, to come to meet you and you must higher yours. Simple words and simple truths are your trademark. It is very difficult to write about our reality."

I watched him leave.

I was back in my room with my book on my lap. I didn't tell anyone; my logical mind wouldn't let me. I worried about being locked up.

Over the following weeks, Simon came many times and brought me to a library with gas lights. He taught me how to organise a small selection of my experiences into the book that you are reading now.

+ + +

A woman phoned me for a reading. She couldn't make her way to Dublin and could we please make an arrangement to do it on the phone?

"Your father John is already here," was my reply. "He is showing me his throat; he is saying his

93

oesophagus is where the problem was. I can see very dark patches through it."

"Yes! That's right. Can I get a pen and write this all down? I wasn't expecting anything now."

"Of course."

John gave her names to add to her page: "Joseph, Edward and Patrick."

"They are my brothers," said the voice on the phone, excited.

"He is showing me where he is from, where he grew up in Ireland. It is very beautiful, picturesque and near the Shannon. He grew up on a dairy farm. I can see a gramophone player in the parlour."

And then I was on the farm. But not that day; in another time. His time.

I could smell the outdoor smells. I watched buttermilk being made in churns. I could touch the wet grass.

"He's an Irish speaker. He's speaking to me *as Gaeilge* now. He's frowning, saying that he doesn't like America, particularly 'Tinseltown', as he's calling it."

She laughed.

"That's where I'm calling from. I live here. He never liked it. Never liked that I left."

I could see him in the parlour now, with his arm on the mantelpiece. It was dark outside and there were people gathered in the room; some of them with instruments. But he told them not to play – he didn't want any accompaniment.

He started to sing "The Sally Gardens" in the most

magnificent baritone. I watched him sing the whole song, only feet away from me. I was standing behind a lady in the room, watching, transfixed. He had a remarkable voice.

When he finished, I was standing at a window, looking out at the ocean and the sunrise. John had brought me somewhere else, somewhere very different. It was a different kind of beautiful. The heat, the colours; I knew it wasn't Ireland. He told me it was where Maureen was standing. Now, on the phone, listening to me, a pen in her hand.

I was seeing her view, and her father John standing with her.

"Maureen, your father has taken me here, there – to where you are standing."

I took a breath and described the scene to her.

For a moment, she couldn't speak. She stopped writing.

"You've stopped writing. He is standing behind you. He wants me to tell you that his left hand is on your right shoulder. He often watches this view with you."

Then, quietly: "I miss him so much. To know he is here . . . watching what I'm doing, looking at the sea with me . . ."

Her voice trailed off. I said goodbye.

✝ ✝ ✝

I got a letter of gratitude in the post from Maureen a couple of weeks later. And for months after that, I had many calls from people in Tinseltown, so I think she was pleased.

+ + +

A young woman rang from America.

No sooner had I said hello to her than I was standing in her home.

"I am in your home, where you are."

Silence.

I sounded like a crazy lady. I don't know why she didn't hang up.

"Don't be frightened. Your husband Paul has brought me there. He wants to be there with you while I speak to you for him. Please don't feel that I am invading your privacy. I can only see you, your house, because he has brought me there. Because he trusts me to speak with you; he allows it. When he wishes it, I will be back in my own home."

Silence.

I ploughed on.

"You are sitting on the sofa. He won't though, not properly. He says he never did. He is sitting on the arm of it, smoking and looking at you now."

"That is exactly how he sat."

"He is there now. Smiling. He said to tell you that the new cushions are beautiful."

"Oh Jesus! I got them last week."

"He likes them. He watched you choose them. He doesn't want to dwell on his passing but, so that you trust that it is him, he is telling me that he had a very rare form of cancer. It was very unusual; the doctors didn't seem to understand it and there was nothing they could do for him. He was fed up having tests done."

She started to cry.

"Yes, that's true. And he is here?"

"Yes, I'm looking at him."

Through me, the couple spoke to each other for some time; a private and intimate conversation.

And then I was back in my kitchen. And the dog running in circles, waiting for me to walk him.

**+ + +**

A woman called Christina phoned for a reading.

"Your mother is here; she's showing me Germany. A map of Germany."

"She lived there for a while."

"She has beautiful skin, dark hair and is very well dressed. She's clutching her chest with her hand. She passed over very suddenly with a heart condition. Mary. Her name is Mary."

"That's Mum."

"She is very anxious that you hear the names John and Thomas."

"They are my brothers, her sons."

"She died in September."

"Oh my God."

"She is showing me divorce papers. She lived alone;

her husband is with another woman. She says he broke her heart."

"Yes."

"I'm in her home; there's a bureau in the hall. It's a beautiful apartment in America. It's warm here. I can hear people outside on the street. I can see the bank from here. It's called The Capital Bank. I can see the sign outside. I have a headache now. It's your mother's headache. She is unhappy with the bank."

Silence.

I waited a moment.

Then, quietly: "We are having problems with that bank. To do with her affairs, sorting her financial affairs, since she died. I can't believe it."

Mary spoke about her grandchildren. And then I was in Switzerland.

"Your father was born in Switzerland. I am standing outside his house."

"Yes!"

I described his home, the area. I was on the move again. I could see the caller now.

"You are sitting on the couch – it's the couch that she bought. I can see you on it, by the window."

"Oh my God."

✦ ✦ ✦

In the next life, you "think" and then you "are". If you "think" you are in Miami, then you "are" there, transported there. The spirits have that freedom. They are unlimited in terms of time and space. And sometimes, to prove their existence to those they love, they will transport me.

A woman sat in front of me. Her husband appeared immediately from the spirit world to speak with her. He didn't hang around. He gave his name and then we were both – he and I – in Croke Park.

I was sitting in the stand. He was in the stand opposite me. He was standing up, wearing a suit. He threw something into the air. As it fell, he whacked it with a hurley. Whatever it was that he hit, I saw it break-up into pieces, dust, and scatter onto the pitch.

I was back in my room. I told his wife what had happened.

"Say no more. That's him all right. Before he died, he asked that he be cremated and his ashes be scattered in Croke Park."

**+ + +**

Now, bilocating is very much a part of my life, of my days. It happens often; I am transported to places near and far and although I find it difficult to understand it, I accept it as part of my work.

# SEVEN

## THE DE LIMAS

I remember the first day I heard Martha's voice. Broken English spoken with beautiful velvety tones.

"May I please speak to Margaret Brazil?"

Brazil. Pronounced beautifully, as in the South American country. And not made to rhyme with razzle, as it does usually.

"This is she."

"My name is Martha de Lima. I am phoning from Paris."

"How can I help you, Martha?"

"My friend has been to see you and has spoken about you so much since. I feel I would love to come to see you."

"Erm, okay . . . Will you be in Ireland soon?"

"Well, yes. I will be in Ireland to see you. I will come

for an appointment. An appointment with you. You tell me when the appointment is, and I will be there. I can fly over in one day and fly back."

*Jesus, Mary and Joseph.* Someone was prepared to fly from Paris for a reading with me. For an "appointment".

I started to fumble for my diary, doing my best to ignore the weight of the pressure descending on my shoulders. I shouldn't have left my cigarettes in the kitchen.

With all the confidence and nonchalance I could inject into my voice – "Hold on, Martha, while I look at my availability . . . I'm free on Friday week, if that would be any good for you?"

"That is wonderful, thank you. I cannot wait. My friend knows where you live so she will drive me. What time is my appointment?"

She had a way of making our arrangement sound so terribly official that really worried me. Did she envisage an orderly, formal set-up with appointment cards and waiting rooms and Spirit Consultancy Suites? I wondered how she'd take my smoky little front room with its wicker chairs and wood-chip walls.

"3.00 p.m."

"I just cannot wait. I shall be there. Thank you, Margaret Brazil."

I put the phone down. Coming from Paris to see me. A woman was coming from Paris to Clondalkin to listen to me. It was at once flattering and utterly terrifying.

+ + +

The day of The Appointment finally arrived. The bell sounded at the Appointed Time.

I opened the door to a tall, stunning woman with porcelain skin. She had long, silky black hair. Everything about her screamed (albeit very politely) money and good living. She had the most beautiful presence. Such a vision on my doorstep did nothing to ease my nerves.

And that was before I clapped eyes on the exquisitely wrapped gift she was holding out toward me.

I reluctantly unwrapped the perfect, bow-tied box to reveal the most intricate and delicate bottle that I had ever seen. A bottle of Parisian perfume.

I responded by immediately asking her when her flight home was.

The only defence I can offer for such rudeness was that I needed to know when this would be over. I thought I might fall to the ground, so great was the pressure of all this beauty and *expectation*.

I brought her into the little room, fighting the urge to apologise for everything in it and to lie about it currently being in the midst of a thorough renovation.

She smiled, and her teeth were dazzling.

But her eyes: her eyes let her down. They were big and round and sad.

She sat patiently while I explained how I worked,

and how I couldn't promise her anything but that I would certainly try my best.

I took her hand for a moment and almost instantly her grandmother appeared; I could see her face, her soft gingery-coloured hair, her shape.

I could have kissed the old lady for her efficiency and clarity.

I relayed what I could see, and Martha and I both relaxed.

"She is your father's mother and she is holding a grape in the palm of her hand. Actually, no, sorry – I think it's an olive. Yes, an olive. She is holding it up now."

"Her name is Olive."

Olive spoke at length about Martha's childhood, and about the house where she had lived; a big, old white house with roses in the gardens.

She showed me photos of Martha in glamorous gowns and told me that she had been a model. It transpired that a series of difficult and sad events had occurred in Martha's life and her spirit had been crushed.

When Olive was finished speaking, she came toward Martha and gave her a huge hug. Martha reacted immediately.

"I feel different. I feel cold. There is something against me."

"This is your grandmother's energy. I am watching her hugging you."

Another figure started to form beside her.

"I can see a thin lady with dark skin. She is wearing a long skirt and I see her walking where there are lots of trees. She is standing quietly by your grandmother. I am waiting for her name clearly – it's Leonora. Her name is Leonora."

She gasped.

"Leonora. My old friend Leonora."

"She is coming toward you with small flowers – they're herbs actually; I can smell them."

"This is her. She grew herbs and made tonics for people with grasses from her garden."

"I can see she is a very spiritual person and a healer herself. She is here to encourage you to live a more spiritual life. She wants you to know that when it is your time, you will develop yourself and unveil your own gift."

Over the next hour or so, Martha de Lima heard exactly what she needed to help her to heal. She was glowing when we finished. Her eyes were big and round and hopeful now. The sadness had left her gaze and she appeared transformed. We talked for a while about healing, about the spiritual dimension to our lives, about my work – doing readings, facilitating healing sessions between people and the spirits. Having come such a distance to see me, I was delighted that I could be of help to this lovely woman.

Martha was visibly happier when we stood again on my doorstep. As for me; I was walking on air. This time I could breathe as I shook her hand. The end was in sight. I even had the presence of mind to remember my manners.

"Goodbye, Martha. And thank you for the beautiful gift. It has been a real pleasure to meet you and I hope you have found what you came here hoping for. Have a safe trip home."

"I want to come back for a healing."

"Goodbye now."

"When can you see me for healing?"

I wasn't hearing things. She did want to come again. I explained to her that everything I did was healing, like her reading today, that she had no reason to make such a journey again, but she wasn't for turning. She wanted to come again, specifically for a healing session.

"I want to book for three healing sessions."

*Three?! I shouldn't have opened my bloody mouth about the healing sessions.*

"Well, I don't think it would be feasible, Martha. I mean, you can't have them three days in a row. I like to allow time in between for the energy to permeate, to see how you feel, to decide what you think you need. It would mean you coming three times . . . I'm sure someone in Paris could help you?"

"If you will give me three appointments . . ." *There was that word again.* ". . . I will come for my *three appointments*. I was led here to you and now that Leonora has come through, I know that she will help me also. I need to do this."

"I see. Well, let me check my diary to see if I have any availability."

As if I didn't have time to get down my stairs to see

a woman who could make her way from France.

The truth was, I didn't have the confidence to see her again. Leave well enough alone. She was happy now. I'd got through it and hadn't disappointed her. I couldn't bear to have her come all this way again and go to all that expense, when I had no control over whether or not it would be a success. I am always at the mercy of the spirits and I can never know what will happen. I can't plan ahead or prepare. I don't know how these things happen. I am just a vehicle. Maybe nothing would happen.

*Jesus Christ. Please have her think the better of this when she gets home. Please. Whoever led her here, please bloody well lead her to someone in her own city.*

So back down the hall I go to consult my little diary, leaving Martha standing outside on the step. My manners had left me again.

+ + +

Two weeks later, Martha de Lima started her healing sessions.

I opened the door to her, in all her French elegance, bearing another festooned gift box.

I wanted to run out the back door in my inferior shoes.

Inside the box, nestled in beautiful pink paper, was a "Rose Candle from Paris". My favourite scent.

"Thank you. Did you have a nice trip?"

"It was the best trip I ever had. I was so excited to get here, to see you, to experience these miracles."

So we began the healing.

The room was warm and Martha lay up on the healing couch in her bare feet. I began to open up her centres so that she would be able to receive whatever healing came in for her. As I began to bring her spirit up through the levels, I saw Olive again. She told me that she had tried to give Martha guidance when she was alive but that Martha had chosen a different path for herself and that through the people she met in modelling and glamour and the choices she made, she had lost herself.

I relayed this to Martha and she understood it. The tears ran down her face.

About an hour later, Martha came to.

"I cannot get off this couch. I have been to heaven. Can I tell you an experience? I have been to the most beautiful place I have ever seen in my life and it is not on this earth. I have been to many countries and lived many places, but I know that this beauty, the colours, the people I have just seen, were from another dimension. They were all wearing white. I wanted to stay there and to never leave. I saw a man and when he looked at me I could tell he knew me, and knew my feelings. I wanted to jump into his arms and never leave."

It was Martha's heart that needed to be healed. And over her three sessions – once a fortnight for the next six weeks – it was.

+ + +

She stood in my garden to leave on that final day.

"I feel so different. I am different now. Different to who I was two months ago when we first met. I'm feeling happy. I'm sleeping so peacefully now. I am at peace with myself. Thank you, Margaret Brazil. Can I keep in contact with you?"

"Of course."

And I meant it. I was actually sorry to see the back of her beautiful frame.

I need not have worried.

That day, twelve years ago, was to be the end of Martha de Lima and me. But it was only the beginning.

+ + +

I had forgotten about Martha, as life was busy; the phone rang, people found me, spirits came. I was learning so much, juggling my children and my home life and trying to control the age-old feelings of anxiety and fear.

*What if today is the day that I am humiliated and the spirits don't come?*

But that feared day never came because the spirits always did.

+ + +

The phone rang.

"Hello, Margaret. This is Martha de Lima. I came to see you from Paris last year? I pray for you every night. I am happy and content like never before. I am moving to Milan with my husband. Maybe when I get settled, you will come to visit me there."

*I don't have the wardrobe to set foot in Milan.*

"Yes, maybe. Thank you."

"Will you please say a prayer that we find the right house for us?"

And with that, I could see the beautiful, big house that they would buy. I described it to her – every little detail; its terracotta colour, the old wooden doors, the shuttered windows, the fireplaces, the vista from the balconies running around the upstairs, and its position in the town.

+ + +

Two weeks later.

"Hello, Margaret. This is Martha de Lima."

"Martha, hello."

"You are amazing. We found the exact house that you described! We have bought it and are going to move in soon. Thank you. I know we will be happy there. That this is the house for us."

"I'm so glad, Martha. Goodbye."

+ + +

A month passed, and then . . .

"Hello, Margaret. This is Martha de Lima."

The same greeting, but a different voice – a different

tone. Martha was crying, hysterical; I couldn't make sense of what she was trying to say.

"Martha, slow down. Take a breath."

"I had a bad fall on the staircase and I have broken bones in my spine. I am in such pain, but the doctors say that I have to rest in bed for many months. I can't afford this with all the expense of the new house and the planned move. Who will mind my boys?"

"Go to bed, Martha. And try to rest. Don't think ahead or worry about what is to come. One day at a time. I will send you healing every day. Have faith, Martha."

As soon as I got off the phone, I went into my healing room and pictured exactly where her pain was. I emptied my mind of my own life, my own challenges, and focused directly on her spine. I could see the whole area at the base of her spine was inflamed. I could see spirits placing their fingers around the broken bones. I saw her lying on her tummy with the base of her spine exposed, and a beautiful gold liquid being poured in around it. I knew in my heart that Martha would experience this healing and that her back would heal quickly.

I did this healing every day, and on the fifth day . . .

"Hello Margaret. This is Martha de Lima."

"Martha, hello."

"I cannot believe it. It is a miracle. I have no pain. I have to take things slowly, but I can walk. I can bend. I can mind my boys, I will be able to get our new house ready. I thought I would be laid up for six months and I would be in traction. But I am well, so fast. I want to ask you if you would come to Milan? Please, Margaret. It would be my gift to you. It would be a joy to have you here."

"That is terribly kind of you, Martha."

"We will take very good care of you. You will be treated like a queen."

Ridiculous negative thoughts swarmed around my head: *I'd need to buy clothes, get toiletries, organise a decent suitcase. It's all too much hassle.* Travelling was so foreign to me, literally.

"You have nothing to worry about, Margaret. We will meet you and look after you. You can do whatever you like when you get here. Please say you'll come. I love you, Margaret."

*Oh my God.*

"I'd have to make arrangements. And I'll have to think about it. And, you know, see if I'm free . . ."

"Of course. Think about it and I will then book your ticket for you. I will call you in three days to see your decision. Goodbye."

I was stunned that a person who had come from Paris for a reading and some healing would fly me to Italy for a holiday. I had barely travelled, and never alone. How will I get to the airport? Where do I collect my ticket? Will she want to spend every day with me? She'll probably want me to do readings for all her friends. Should I eat with the family? I had a look at a map. It looked like there were mountains. Not what I imagined. *It's too foreign for me. Even thinking about it has me worked up. I won't go.*

**+ + +**

Two weeks later, I met Martha de Lima at Milan's Malpensa airport.

I was carrying a bag containing gifts that seemed a good idea when I'd bought them hours before in Dublin Duty Free – a loaf of brown bread and a pot of strawberry jam. Now, in the back of a Mercedes Benz, driving through the most wondrous scenery, they seemed very out-of-place.

The warmth of the welcome of Martha's family was quite astonishing – the two boys, her husband, their home help. When we arrived into the grounds in the house, I was awestruck. It was monstrous, splendid. Every wing had balconies bedecked with flowers.

My room was cream and powder blue. And filled with white roses. The bed was home to what seemed like a hundred little silk cushions. I resolved to enjoy every minute of my stay.

Martha and I took a lot of walks and spoke about healing and the spirit world over the few days. I showed her exercises that she could do to relax her mind and open herself up to healing and to contact from the spirits. How to let her mind wander into truth and to sharpen her intuition.

We talked about how to feel energy, how distant healing works, how there are no boundaries in the spirit world – no gates, no barbed wire; how someone does not have to be physically present with me for them to feel the healing touch that comes from the higher level through me.

When I look out and see cars, I can see the power – the energy, tiny sparks of light – moving around them. Even a traffic jam can be enhanced if you can see the energy! Everything sparkles – we sparkle – and when we die, our body decays but our soul, our essence, still sparkles, like thousands of tiny stars.

Martha's grandmother made regular appearances during our chats, and would give names and messages to Martha that would give her great evidence and comfort.

Martha was like a sponge, absorbing everything over those days. Her aura shone and danced with bright gold light. In those few days, she learned some of the principles and lessons that it had taken me years to discover for myself. Life had come back into Martha's spirit. She was giddy like a child with a new, precious possession – something that would always be a comfort.

✦ ✦ ✦

Martha had a housekeeper from the Philippines. Her name was Eileen. One afternoon as I sat in the kitchen, I could see her father standing behind her. And then her brother.

"Eileen, I don't want to give you a fright but your father is standing behind you. He is allowing me to see him so I think he's happy for me to tell you this."

"Oh my goodness! My father!?"

She blessed herself.

"Yes, he has passed over. He is a small man with a very wide smile. Also, next to him is your brother. They are together in the next life."

In an instant, I found myself in a little village, thronged with people. I saw a little boy and a man with him. I could tell that they were both living. That this was the present, and they were in the Philippines. I described them both to Eileen and gave her their names.

"This is my husband and son. I am hoping that I can save enough to get them over here. I want us to make our lives here in Italy."

I met them both many years later, in Italy. But my first time to see them was an out-of-body experience when I stood briefly next to them in the Philippines.

+ + +

I returned home. Many months passed.

"Hello, Margaret. This is Martha de Lima. My mother and father want to come and see you."

"They live in South America, don't they . . . ?"

*Please don't let this be going where I fear it might be going.*

"Yes. They are going to come from Colombia to see you. If you give them a time and date they will be there, if you will see them."

*Oh dear God.*

"Of course. That would be fine."

Two hours elapsed . . .

"Hello, Margaret. This is Eduardo de Lima."

*Mother of God.*

"We want to come to see you when it's convenient for you."

*Christ!*

He went on. He had to, the silence was deafening.

"You have helped our daughter so much. We want to come to see you. Are you available to see us at any time?"

*Good God. Jesus. People coming from South America.*

I was cursing Martha and her fantastic hospitality. I couldn't even begin to compete with that. But I was going to have to make an effort for her parents in my home.

+ + +

One Saturday in May, a well-dressed elderly couple knocked on my door hoping to speak to spirits, having found their way to Clondalkin in West Dublin from Cali in Colombia.

Still now, it makes me laugh when I think about it.

I brought Helena into the sitting room to wait, as Eduardo had opted to have his reading first. An attractive and charming lady, originally from Baltimore in the US, she politely ignored my West Highland terrier periodically charging down the garden and banging his body against the glass doors, trying to get back in.

Eduardo sat with me. His mother came through to speak immediately.

A man stood behind her – his father. A healthy-looking man with grey hair.

"He is a small man. Standing at a huge table covered in papers, books, files, bits of papers everywhere. Books line all of the shelves. Ernest. His name is Ernest. A very content man."

"My father, Ernest, he was a writer."

And with that Eduardo's mother came right up into my face to talk. I described her clothes – plum-coloured cardigan, black skirt – the way she held her arms, her mannerisms and her grand gestures as she spoke.

The tears were in Eduardo's eyes. The reading went on and his parents spoke very clearly to him about his other daughter Christina, about whom he worried endlessly. After some time, I was told to put my hand over his heart.

I heard myself say, "Eduardo, you have a health problem. Your parents are not telling you anything that you don't know. It's not my job to be the bearer of bad tidings. You are a doctor. Your heart – your heart is not healthy. But you know that?"

"Yes, I do. I have a problem with my heart."

He had his legs crossed and was sitting rigidly on the chair.

"Please try to relax and uncross your legs. Let your body relax into the chair. You are going to block any energy coming to you if you are resistant to it or your body is closed."

And he did. Eduardo relaxed and spent the next hour receiving healing and wonderful evidence from his parents.

"I had to come to hear you with my own ears. I could not believe it, believe in you. Until now."

+ + +

I don't remember much about Helena's reading. I do recall that her father John came through very quickly. He had great compassion for her for leaving her home and going to live in South America. I could see her singing in the church choir, and then I saw her mother – a very heavy woman, lying in a bed but not at home. In a room being cared for; a rest home.

I felt myself connect with this elderly woman's spirit, yet I could tell she was still alive.

"Your mother is alive, but she is unwell. I can speak with her spirit but I know she has not yet passed over."

Helena gasped. Tears ran down her face.

"My mother has lived with Alzheimer's for many years. She has not communicated with anyone at all in a very long time. She does not know me."

"She does know you. Her spirit knows you very well."

I spoke to Helena about her mother, her mother's memories of times they shared. She was overwhelmed.

+ + +

Afterwards, Eduardo, Helena and I chatted for hours into the night. We had a very natural and easy rapport. I have no idea where they were staying but they left in a cab to go there at two o'clock in the morning.

+ + +

A year passed . . .

"Hello, Margaret. This is Martha de Lima."

She was crying about her father. He was being taken into hospital to have a heart operation.

"I will put the phone down and immediately send him some absent healing. His mother is standing here; she tells me he is very frightened but that he will be fine. The surgery will not be as serious as he is expecting. Tell your dad that he need not feel fearful; I will be with him at the hospital and I will hold his hand through the procedure."

This was not my ego speaking, or my feeling like I had special powers. I was told to say this, that indeed I would be with him, and that hearing this would go some small way toward easing the man's anxiety.

Meditation and healing can be done anywhere. I sat on the chair next to the phone and cleared my mind. I always speak to Jesus for healing. He is my guiding light. I asked for help for Eduardo de Lima.

Immediately, I was in a hospital in Colombia. I could see everything very vividly; Eduardo was one of two men in a room waiting. They were both sitting up in their beds, the blue-green curtains between them hanging open. He was in the bed nearest the corridor, wearing a silk dressing gown. I saw people arrive to bring him to the theatre. I took his hand and prayed. My mind and spirit were there, listening to the Spanish voices. I went into the theatre with him.

And then I was back in my hallway.

I phoned Martha back. She confirmed the detail of the room. And the fact that he had just been brought down for surgery.

But then . . .

"No. No. He doesn't have a silk dressing gown. He has a woollen one; I bought it."

"Well I have seen him, clearly, in a patterned silk gown today. And I know that the operation will be less than he fears; they will not do the more serious surgery. He will end up just having a small procedure."

I think she was thrown by my getting the dressing gown wrong. Her voice sounded anxious as we said our goodbyes.

✚ ✚ ✚

"Margaret, Margaret. This is Martha de Lima. Everything you said was correct. My father is out of theatre and they did not do the major surgery. He just had a small procedure – an angioplasty, with a local anaesthetic – and he is back in his bed sending emails. I asked him what dressing gown he was wearing. He said he had been given a present of a lovely, patterned silk one and he was wearing it because it was lighter. He had put his woollen one back in the bag."

+ + +

A year later . . .

"Hello, Margaret. This is Martha de Lima. My father is unwell. The pain is very bad this time. It is getting worse."

Straight away, I was at the hospital and I saw a team of surgeons, specialist doctors discussing Eduardo's case.

"Doctors are discussing your father's condition. He will be going to North America – Washington, I think – to have surgery. It seems that this is the best solution for now. Don't worry. He will be okay on the flight. He should take lots of aspirin. I'm not a doctor, Martha, so I don't understand this but I am being told that he will be having four stents put in around his arteries. The world is not ready to let him go yet. He will recover very well and quickly. And he will be as good as new after this."

And he was. He went to Washington, where cardiologists put four stents in, and he flew home to Colombia within a fortnight. This was nearly ten years ago.

+ + +

Eduardo and Helena were kidnapped in Colombia on Sunday, 17th September 2000.

A hooded gang with guns took them and other

members of their family from near their home in the highlands outside the city of Cali. Martha phoned me as soon as she heard, demented with fear and worry. I told her I would phone her back with any information I had.

"Martha, your dad is fine. I am communicating with his energy. He is alive. And he will be found today. He is exhausted but he is okay."

About four or five hours later, she phoned me again.

"Oh, Margaret! They have just found him. He had been left on the side of the mountain because of his heart condition. He couldn't keep up. He is traumatised and very tired, but he is well. He is very lucky that he wasn't shot."

I prayed for Helena, who was being held captive. I knew that she was still alive. I could see a dirty shack, with broken wooden steps outside it where she was being held, blindfolded.

"Martha, your mother is alive. She is being held, blindfolded, but no harm is coming to her. She will be returned home safely to you soon."

Martha left Milan and went to Colombia.

The following day, the police descended on a shack high in the mountains of southwest Colombia. It was reported that a female, American citizen was among the hostages freed. Martha was there with her father when Helena was returned safely to them that evening.

+ + +

Eighteen months ago, Martha phoned to say she was going to Colombia because her father had taken a bad turn. "He is in his own hospital, the hospital where he works. The staff and his patients have candles lighting for him."

"It is not up to me, Martha. It is God's will, but I will send him absent healing. They will not be moving him elsewhere for surgery this time. He is not well enough."

I knew that this time things were more serious. Eduardo's mother showed me that the part of the artery needing repair was difficult to access. But that it would work – that it would be successful. He would no longer be in pain and he would recover well.

Again, Eduardo was home within days.

He is still well. And he still flies to Milan to visit Martha. I have told him that he won't be leaving this world for a while because it'll take me some time to save for the fare to Colombia and the spirits wouldn't let me miss his send-off. The day I come into funds, maybe he should start to worry!

# Eight

## Uninvited Guests

From my experiences, I would say that spirits are never here to "haunt" a house. I think the verb is mistakenly attributed to them by people who misunderstand their intentions and their circumstances.

It is true that, from time to time, spirits don't cross over into the light. People who have made their peace, who maybe have had a chance to prepare for their death; they are lucky and their souls will usually go over into the light in an instant. Without hesitation. Others are not so lucky.

There are various reasons why a spirit may not pass over easily. It might be because they died very suddenly – perhaps in a collision or an accident – and are in a kind of shock themselves. They can be disorientated. Looking on with everyone else gathered around the wreckage of the car. They feel no pain but the shock is real. And it can be severe. Their first thought might be to go home, or to some other familiar place. They will resist the light, because they're bewildered. When they come around, they may be back in their own house or perhaps with someone they knew, someone they felt comfortable with. Back here in this world, but without their physical selves.

Suicide victims can sometimes get stuck here as a result of feelings of uncertainty about what they've done and fear about what the consequences of their action might be. Fearing "hell", these spirits sometimes choose to "stick" here, to go nowhere. They choose not to move on.

On occasion, the spirit of a person who dies in dreadful pain can become overwhelmed by the experience and a part of that spirit will hold on to the memory of the pain. The spirit will be lost, disjointed and unable to join the rest of the soul. To pass on, the spirit will need to let go of the horror, the strength of the memory. It may simply need time or it may need "rescuing" to go over to the next life.

At times, extreme stubbornness can prevent a spirit from passing on. Spirits who are very wilful, perhaps with an addictive personality, can remain here. Just as they might have an addiction to alcohol or another substance, they can similarly be addicted to ownership; to their lifestyle, their property, their possessions. Some people are completely attached to what they own and this can make it difficult for them to leave with nothing. They haven't learned that we can never really own anything in this life. That we only "use" what we have and then we leave it behind and somebody else "uses" it. They become stuck as they're so reluctant to move on, to let go of their belongings, their strong personality, their earthly life.

The light is brightness, an invitation, an infusion of all of the earthly colours. It represents Higher Knowledge and is an overwhelming feeling of unconditional love. Everything is a choice, so when the day comes and we find ourselves no longer attached to our bodies, to this life, we will choose to go towards the outstretched welcoming light – or not. Most do. But it is possible to resist it. I believe that it's never the case that these souls don't want to go toward the light. They do see it, but their fear or shock or whatever it is they feel remains vivid in their memory and prevents them reaching for it. Over the years I have had to encourage and coerce and even drag some of them toward the brightness. They don't realise that they're doing any harm here; that they may be in the way, that their presence is upsetting the living. When the body is gone, only the spirit and the mind remain. And that means they are timeless entities. Without the body, without the physical life, there is no routine, no structure – no time to go to work, time to get up, time to go to bed. They don't know that they've been months or years in the one house; sitting in a bedroom, standing in the kitchen.

Spirits don't resolve to "haunt" a house and

terrorise the people in it. That is not their intention. They are just souls who are lost and stuck here for a time, but they can be brought, with great gentleness, to the Divine light where they find peace, where they belong. In my experience, most souls who have difficulty passing over are worried about "facing their Maker", as it was put in my day. And that is a terrible shame. God is light; there is no judgement there, only help. But these spirits are usually judging themselves.

+ + +

Many years ago when I had only just started doing readings for people, a young mother, Rachel, phoned me. Her six-year-old daughter Melissa was experiencing "weird things and seeing spirits". The child would describe the very minutiae of people – one young boy on a bicycle, in particular – that she could see and she complained of hearing noises coming from her wardrobe. The parents dismissed these things as childhood fantasy and fears.

That was until the child's very level-headed and cynical father saw a spirit in sackcloth pass him on the stairs one evening.

He started to take Melissa more seriously. The spirit of the young boy that the child claimed to see accompanied her most places, once she left the house. Walking down the street with her mother, Melissa would describe him and his bike and what he was doing. The mother mentioned it to friends in the area whom she trusted not to think her insane. It transpired that a young boy of Melissa's age had lived on her street some years previous and was killed when he was hit by a car cycling back to his house.

Now Rachel was taking them both seriously.

The parents grew increasingly anxious about it all, as did Melissa herself. She didn't want to see this boy, or the bigger men, or to hear these banging noises, these cries. These were not imaginary friends.

I listened to the mother tell me all of this on the phone. I felt her anxiety and she sounded like a very sincere person, but I didn't know what I could do.

"Give me your address. I'll come up to your house and . . ."

I didn't know how to finish the sentence. I didn't know what the hell I was going to do when I got there.

"Thanks so much. That would be great. We don't know what to do."

*You're in good company so.*

+ + +

I went to the house a few days later. I had no fear or trepidation about going in, about what I might stumble across there, because I had no plan to do anything. I had just come to try to give the woman some peace of mind so she could comfort her daughter.

I spoke to Melissa, a dark curly-haired angel, about this and that. As I would to any six-year-old.

All of a sudden, I could see her aura. A huge, wide

light halo around her body. I could see the top of her aura; the light was very wide and open. It did not close around her head as most people's would – like the halo you might see around a saint in a picture. I could tell that this little girl could indeed see people who had passed on, that she was not closed down and rooted in this world.

She went skipping out the back door to play.

I sat down with her mother.

"Rachel, before we talk about what might be going on in the house, I have to tell you that Melissa's mind energy – her aura – is wide open. The only thing that I can do is close her down so that she won't be seeing these spirits. She is too young to cope with it and I know it is scaring you and her."

"I don't care what it takes. Please do it. I just want a little girl who can go to school, play with her friends and sleep easy at night."

"People like Melissa do have a special gift – I don't know how it happens – but at her age the best thing to do is for her to be closed down. I will close her down, with God's permission and will, but ask that if it is her gift to share with others in her life then He will open her up again, like a flower, when she is older – at the appropriate and best age for her and others."

Melissa came back in. I spoke to her again. While I was talking to her, I was asking her own angels and her own guides to close her down. Because she was too young to do it for herself. There was no big rigmarole. I just prayed for her as we chatted. I saw her aura get smaller and smaller until a tiny little bud of light at the top of her head was all that was left. I can see it so clearly now as I recall it. As she skipped off again, I was very doubtful. This was uncharted territory for me and I wasn't sure if I had the right to do this, to close down someone's gift. I did the best that I could and what I hoped was for the best for the child and her family.

I asked to be shown to the room where Melissa was hearing the sounds come from the wardrobe. I had a candle, an incense stick and my rosary beads. What I was going to do, I had no idea. I asked Michael the Archangel to come in and cleanse the room. I sat on the bed with my eyes closed, praying for this family. In a split second, I could hear noises – horses and carts and voices – and then I could see bonfires in the darkness. I could make out soldiers, an encampment. I could see the horses were drawing the carts, and hanging over the sides were the legs of dead or injured men.

I knew that the presences, the sounds, were not coming from within the house. That they were from the area. I was told to bless every corner of the room, which I did. When I was finishing, the wardrobe door opened and slammed shut.

*Holy Jesus Christ and Mother of God! WHAT am I doing here?!*

I nearly jumped out of my skin.

I asked my own guides what was going on. I was told that there was a spirit leaving the home. One of these men had lingered from this time. I was instructed to close the portal – in this case the wardrobe.

*The porthole?! Like in a ship?! What's a porthole?*

I have learned now that the residual energy can stay in an area, just like a memory. The spirit that the father had seen on the stairs had lingered on in the area where thousands had died, the land upon which the house had been built.

I had an understanding that spirits who get lost or have traumatic deaths can linger on. They don't quite make it over to the other side. My guides showed me how to seal up the portal in the corner with my mind.

Coming down the stairs, I could see Rachel standing by the back door chewing her nails. She had heard the noises, the crowd sounds, the bang. I stood next to her, next to the door. I said I hoped that I had been able to help. I didn't mention the fact that my legs were wobbling and that I couldn't wait to get out of the place. I did my best to explain what I hoped I had done, but I couldn't fully understand it myself. And it did sound a bit ridiculous out loud.

Rachel told me that the site was a historical battleground, a settlement.

*Jesus Christ.*

She offered me tea. I said I had an appointment.

I was a nervous wreck saying goodbye. I told her to phone me and let me know how Melissa was and how things went. I pulled out of her driveway, parked around the corner and had two cigarettes.

I hoped I had done the right thing. And I sincerely hoped the spirit of a disgruntled soldier wasn't in the back of my car looking for a new place to live.

**+ + +**

Many years passed and I forgot about Melissa and her parents. I had no more dealings with presences in people's homes. Until one day in 2004 when the phone rang.

A lady asked me if I would see her in her house in Finglas. She said she thought that it might be haunted. I went.

I was aware of the spirit of an elderly lady in the home soon after I arrived. I went up the stairs. I had no feeling that the lady had lived in the house. She didn't belong there. Her energy didn't fit with the house. I found myself drawn up to the attic. I felt that she was hiding up there; hiding from me.

I got into the attic and sat down. She was there. I asked her to tell me her name.

"Mary. But everyone calls me May."

"Did you live here?"

"No."

"Why are you here now?"

"I'm here to help the poor woman downstairs. She's going through what I went through in my life. I want to help her. She needs me here, for support."

"It's lovely that you want to help. But you being here isn't helping. It's time for you to leave, May, for you to relax. You had your life and now you should be at rest, reaping the rewards."

She was silent.

I knew what I had to do. During my meditations, I had often seen a bridge connecting this world and the next. It was beautiful, with colours more vivid and alive than we can imagine here on our limited earth. I could see the energy of spirits at the end of this bridge; joyful and inviting. I knew that May needed rescuing, that she belonged in that world now.

"I have come here today to bring you by the hand to a bridge. I'll take you there. When you get there, everyone that you've ever loved will be there waiting for you on the other side. Anyone that you don't want to be there, won't be."

The two louvered doors in a press at the back of the attic flung open and then slammed shut. Open, slam, open, slam.

May was rebelling. She didn't want to go.

I put my left hand out.

"May, I will get help for the lady downstairs. I feel that she had no choice but to leave her situation and her previous home. Now she has moved to this house with her children for some peace and some normality. For a new start. I promise to help her. But you must go. I know you think that you're doing the right thing, but you're actually scaring them all. They aren't sleeping. They're afraid to go up the stairs. I know this isn't what you intended. Do you think that's fair on them?"

I stretched my hand toward her further.

I could see this small, well-meaning lady; her energy on my left hand.

We didn't have to walk anywhere in the physical

sense. She is a spirit with no body. Mentally, I took her to a meadow and a bridge came into sight; a bridge with coloured lights, every colour of the rainbow. I knew it as soon as I saw it. And an amazingly blue little river below. I felt tears as she approached the bridge, tears on my face, but they were not mine. May's tears. She was feeling anxious, worried that she wasn't good enough. That the people she loved wouldn't be there for her. I felt the grip on my hand tighten.

"It's not my time yet, May. I can't go over with you. I will hold your hand on the bridge until you feel confident enough to go yourself. When you let go, I will keep watching you. I promise not to take my eyes off you until you see your family, and you get home."

She continued over the bridge and our hands parted.

I saw her mother, her friends and a young child of hers that had died. They circled her. Then a group of friends came to her. So much light. I felt tears now, but they were my own. I stood and watched and waited for her to turn, to wave me on, to say goodbye.

She turned, smiled and waved. She was happy to go with them.

I brought myself back down the bridge, through the meadow and into my own physicality.

I recounted everything to the nervous lady downstairs. It wasn't a cleansing in this instance, just a clearing out. A rescue, really. The spirit was harmless, a gentle soul just trying to help.

I stood in the kitchen with this lady who had phoned. I explained why May was there. Why she empathised with her. How she knew about her pain. As I spoke, a beautiful snow white dove – a bird I had previously only ever seen represented in drawings – flew down and stood in front of both of us on the window sill. We were speechless. It lingered, looking back at us for a moment, and then flew away. We both knew that we had received the acknowledgement that we sought; we knew that May was at peace. And that the home would be calm and quiet from now on.

And so it was.

+ + +

"Hello, Margaret? My name is Frances. My sister and I were with you for a reading many years ago. I wonder if you can help me. My house is haunted. It's haunted."

She sounded fairly certain. No question about it.

"What makes you think it's 'haunted'?"

"Things get moved all of the time. The bed gets rattled and shaken. Even if I go up for a nap during the day. They won't let me sleep. There's banging coming from the radiator. Like someone's banging against it. I've had plumbers in to see if the radiators are faulty. But they're not. I knew that. It only happens when I'm in the bedroom. I know it's nothing logical. Sometimes, there's a smell of smoke on the landing, for no reason. The gas keeps being switched on and off. I swear, Margaret, I'm cracking up at this stage."

I asked Frances for her address and said that I'd come up and have a look. I believed her. I asked her to have as many of her family there as possible at the time, so that I could try to get a handle on the situation. On what might be going on in the house.

+ + +

I remember Frances' face when she opened the door.

I went inside. The house was absolutely freezing.

She told me it had been her dream house; she had waited very long for it to come on the market, to secure the sale. They had done it up exactly the way they wanted. She really loved this house. Not long after everything was done and they moved in, these disturbances started. There were cold spots in the house where heat simply could not penetrate, no matter how high the thermostat was turned up. Frances now wanted to move house, even though she and her husband had put everything of themselves into it.

I spoke to her teenage son and daughter to ensure they hadn't brought anything in, or that a negative energy hadn't latched onto them. But I could tell by their auras that they hadn't.

Frances' son didn't say much. She knew he was troubled by the noises and seeing shadows but he didn't like to talk about it. Her daughter had felt somebody standing behind her in the kitchen and a hand on her shoulder. She heard the noises a lot.

They had had the priest in to bless it, but nothing changed. Frances told me I was the family's only hope.

I asked them all to leave while I tuned in to the energy in the rooms. I didn't have to twist their arms. They were out of the house in a flash and I was alone in this unfamiliar house. I asked Michael the Archangel to bless me on my way around the rooms.

I started upstairs in Frances' bedroom as this was where most of the activity was. As soon as I walked through the door, I was brought back in time.

I could see an older baby standing up in a cot. Rattling the side with both hands. I could smell smoke, growing thicker and thicker, until I was suffocating. I knew this child had died in a fire. But not in this house. She didn't belong here. I took her in my arms and told her to clasp her hands around me. I rubbed her back. I told her that I had to work but she could come with me.

"You are going to a wonderful place. And you will never need to rock that cot again."

As I left the room with her, I saw an elderly man in the corner.

"Who are you?"

"I'm Joseph – Frances' father. I'm just here to help you."

"Great, Joseph. Thank you. I need all the help I can get."

Joseph, the little girl and I went into the next room.

The colour changed. Everything was dark and dreary. A man stood against the wall drinking out of a glass. His aura was dark – dark and negative. He was ugly and stubborn. Noxious smells of alcohol filled the room. But the room was different; not like it was now. This was in an earlier time.

*Here we go now. This guy's not going to go without a fight.*

I could see he was totally rooted in his addiction and in staying earthbound.

Before I got a chance to speak, he snarled: "I'm not going anywhere and I'm not giving up the drink for anyone."

*Great.*

"Did you live in this house?"

"Yes, I did."

I asked him his name. He gave it, with a growl.

"Listen, Harry, you have to leave this house today."

"Fuck off."

"There's a young boy who uses this room and you're disturbing him, and that's not allowed. If you're afraid to go over and be judged, that's your problem. You shouldn't make it his problem."

I hoped to appeal to the kinder side of his spirit.

He was arched in the door, adamant, his hand on the architrave, blocking anyone getting in or out. The whole doorway was dark.

I went over and looked him straight in the eye, Michael the Archangel, Joseph and the baby girl with me. There were angels all around; angels for the baby and angels for Harry himself.

"It's time for you to go. You will be leaving here today. We have a dilemma now; we have a child here who was burnt in the fire. She got a fright and needs someone's hand to bring her to the other side. She can't do it alone. You can solve this problem, Harry. You're going to have to help."

With that, the darkness lightened a little, and the coldness became less.

I pressed on.

"Come on now, Harry. You have to come. Look at all the angels. There's nobody here giving out to you or wanting to punish you. They're all here to help you. It's time to go. And it's time for you to step up and help."

So back we all go into Frances' bedroom. I sat on the bed. The angels circled us. I asked for us to be brought to the bridge instantly. I had no concerns about the baby but I was worried about Harry, in case he might change his mind and cause disturbance or refuse to leave the house. I needed to keep him moving, before he had too long to think about it. His energy was strong and obstinate and negative. He would be an aggravating presence in any home.

The thought is the deed, so immediately we were at the bridge.

"Pull yourself together, Harry. We're going to go now. You won't know yourself. You're going to help me too. I need you to get this little girl over. When we get to the top of that bridge there, you might have to take her, and bring her down to her grandparents and anyone else that's there belonging to her."

This time the bridge itself was completely purple. And filled with light. Light soaring up for miles and miles.

Harry and the little child made their way, with Joseph keeping them company. I called after them to wave back at me when they got there, when they reached everyone, when they were home.

I cried like a baby for both of them, watching them brave their journey.

They turned back at the end of the bridge and waved together. I could see spirits crowding around, welcoming them to the other side.

**+ + +**

I came down the stairs with red, bulging eyes. I texted Frances to say it was time to come back. I told her about the child and Harry.

Frances verified that there had been a fire in the house behind them, and that a toddler had lost her life in it. Her son was very relieved to hear about the alcoholic man in his room as he had seen him but didn't want to tell anyone.

"Frances, your father Joseph was in your bedroom and he assisted me in bringing them over. He told me he was here to help."

She smiled. She believed utterly.

"That would be him. He'd travel miles to help a soul."

Knowing that Joseph had been there gave the family great evidence and great peace.

I left, thinking that this would be the end of Frances and her "haunted" house. As far as we were all concerned, peace would reign in this home forever more. We were wrong.

+ + +

Two years later, I got another phone call from Frances.

"Margaret, it's Frances."

I placed her immediately. Her tone was grave.

"Jesus, what?! Don't tell me they're back?"

"There's definitely someone in the house. The noises have started up again. Like before. I can't sleep. The bed's being rattled and shaken. I can't take it anymore."

I felt very disappointed in myself. That I hadn't done a thorough enough job. But there had been no activity in over two years. I couldn't understand it.

Suddenly, I heard the name Christopher.

"Who's Christopher?"

"Christ! I knew him well! Why?"

"He's the person in your house."

"What?! He was found dead a while ago. He had been missing for a few days."

"Well, I can hear him now. He's making contact with me. It's strange that he's in your house though. Bear with me for a minute, Frances . . . He's telling me that he fell into water. It was 'the demon drink' that killed him. He had low self-esteem and no will power. It was a wet night. There were puddles. He knew where he was going, but he was disorientated with the drink. He decided to take a short cut home. These are his words to you directly, Frances: 'I slipped but I wasn't able to save myself. I couldn't find my way home. But I found you. I found you with Carmel.'"

"Carmel?! Jesus Christ and Holy Saint Joseph."

This was obviously of some significance.

"Yes, he's saying that he found you with someone called Carmel on the Thursday."

"Oh fuck off, Margaret. I just can't believe it. I go to Bingo with Carmel every Thursday night, and that's the night he went missing."

"Well, he's saying that he couldn't find his way home that Thursday night recently, but instead he found you and went home with you. He's saying that your 'fucking dogs' frighten him every night."

I had to laugh.

Frances was staggered.

I could see very clearly that Frances had a special gift, that she was a beacon of light for souls. Comparable to a lighthouse for ships in distress. Lost souls were coming toward Frances' light for comfort, to guide them home.

"Jesus, Margaret. You better get up here. I can't go through much more of this."

Frances started shouting into the room behind her: "I'm getting Margaret up to help you. To get you out of here. So you can stop banging around the place. I've heard you. She's coming. Now stop it."

**+ + +**

I went up to the house the following day. This time I asked Frances to stay with me. I felt she needed to learn about her own gift. I invited her to come around the rooms with me.

"You're all right. I'll sit in the garden."

I went up the stairs and saw Christopher straight away in Frances' bedroom. He was in an awful state; crying and fretting. I had to encourage him: "You found Frances so she could help you, and I'm here because she wants to help you. She's not throwing you out. She just wants you to be happy. When you're making noise and trying to get attention, you're upsetting the family. They can't sleep so they can't function the next day."

He sat on the bed beside me. He was wiping his nose with his sleeve, trying to pull himself together.

Michael the Archangel was there and other angels for this lost, frightened soul. I gathered the little band together.

"Come on, everyone. It's time to go."

Christopher started to cry twice as hard. I held him to me.

I asked that we go straight to the bridge.

He saw it immediately, but was disorientated and reluctant. A grown man, he fought the journey every step of the way. He held on to every post, pulling away, wanting to bolt. I reassured him and coaxed him on, my arms around him, wiping his tears. He was still staggering, frightened.

His father appeared suddenly – Thomas. His face

full of compassion. And he took his son over; the man became like a child and his daddy brought him home.

Christopher didn't wave back. He's the only spirit I've ever brought over who didn't. But his father did. He turned back and waved me on as though to say, "Go on. I have him now. He'll be okay."

I brought myself back and asked for a sign that the house was at peace, that the clearance had been executed fully and properly. The loudest chimes, as though from within a Buddhist Temple or a Church ceremony, rang out in the room. Over and out. I stood up.

I went out to the garden where Frances was waiting. After I told her what had happened, we sat for a while in silence. I knew she and I needed to talk further. I felt she knew it too.

"This is going to keep happening. I'm being told that you have a special gift. If this is to be your mission in life, to attract the lost in the spirit world and bring them home to rest, then you need to accept it. I am being told that you can help people who have just passed over and you can also help the dying."

I waited for her to freak out.

She didn't.

"I know you're right. There have been other things that I didn't mention. When I'm in a hospital, I know who's going to die that night. Who's not ever going to go home. Without knowing why they're there or what their story is. I can feel it. And I'm always right. People I don't know anything about, their illnesses or otherwise. People of all ages."

"You are a beam, a white light for the dying and those who have just died."

"I understand what you're saying, but why me? Why don't they fucking go somewhere else?"

"You have to learn how to deal with this, to use your wonderful gift to help."

"No. I can't. I don't want this. I wouldn't be able to do it."

"No harm will come to you. You learn to protect yourself and then you guide these people, these souls. You are doing a great service for them and for yourself. No harm will come to you. You can do this, Frances."

"Okay. If it ever happens again, I'll think about it. But that's probably it for now. You've blessed everything – corners, windows, doors – and the house is quiet. I'd say that's it."

"Yes, there's nothing here now. I heard chimes."

"Goodbye, Margaret. I hope I never see you again."

✚ ✚ ✚

The phone rang six months later.

"Margaret, there's somebody in the house." She barely stopped to draw a breath. "I've been denying it to myself, trying to explain things away, but definitely, there's someone here. There are cold spots in my bedroom, on the landing, and in the kitchen. For the last fortnight, there's been a constant, overpowering smell of aftershave in my room and in my car. Jesus Christ; will they never leave me alone? A neighbour saw a man wearing a green shirt and glasses sitting in front of the TV in the front room. I can't take any more of this house. I thought this was all over. The house alarm is going off, when it isn't even on. Every bulb in the place is blowing. The gas is being turned on, and left on, in the kitchen when there's nobody there. The smell in the place when we get home is unreal. There were sounds – voices – coming from upstairs yesterday. I had to ring you. I know you're sick of me."

"Frances, it's Noel."

Silence.

Then a whisper.

"Noel! Ah stop, Margaret. Stop. I've just been at the church for Noel's funeral mass."

"He has red hair and glasses. He was in your house for two weeks before his death."

"Are you sure!? Jesus."

"He's telling me he lived alone. He was widowed. He had cancer. He's very happy in your house."

"Oh Jesus. Jesus Christ! Margaret. What's he doing here?! What does he want? I don't even know him that well. I was a friend of his sister's."

"Yes, he's nodding. His sister Bernie."

"Fuck!"

"He's smiling."

"Oh Margaret, you'll have to come up. I can't deal with this. He only died on Tuesday but his spirit has been here for the last two weeks. *When he was still alive?!*"

"I don't know, Frances. I'm just relaying what he's saying."

"I've never heard of anything like that."

"You can do this yourself, Frances."

"No, Jesus, no! Not this time. The man *was alive*! Margaret you have to come and get him. I am in shock. The man with the green shirt and the glasses. Sitting here. BEFORE HE DIED."

"I'll come up this afternoon."

**+ + +**

I sat opposite Frances in the house and asked Noel for evidence that it was him and why he was there. I could hear his reply in my mind.

"Initially, I had gastric problems but it transpired that I had cancer in my stomach. When my subconscious mind knew I was in the last stages of life, I slept a lot. My spirit left my body, left the pain. I couldn't cope with dying, the word 'cancer'. I couldn't handle it. I found myself drifting, and then I found Frances. I could see her light. I came straight here. I always loved her laughter when she was friends with Bernie."

This was all new to me. The idea that a spirit could leave its shell, its overcoat, before passing on. I had to put aside my curiosity and my logical mind to help. Help Noel to find his way home, and give Frances back hers.

I went up the stairs to her bedroom. Again. There was her father, standing in the corner. I was delighted to see him.

"We're keeping you busy, Joseph. Thank God you're here."

"Anything I can do to help, Frances."

I needed to find Noel and gain his trust.

"Come on, Noel. It's time for you to go home."

The answer came: "I've no belief in the afterlife. I'm happy to stay here."

"Noel, you lived alone for a long time. Would you have liked someone to come in, turn on your gas, mess with your alarm, squirt aftershave all over the place? You would've run a mile. You're disturbing the peace. You're interfering with this family and upsetting them."

"I'm not in the way."

"You *are* in the way, Noel. You're causing mischief being here and it's not fair. There is a better place for you to go and your wife is waiting there for you. You need to overcome your fear about the next life. You found your way to Frances because she can help you. We're all here to help you; me, your angels, Joseph and Michael the Archangel. We're all going to take you over to the next world. Come with me."

I could see him start to pack a little brown case. That was him. Neat and tidy. Still trapped in the physical. Tears ran down his face. He locked his case and stood up with it in his hand. He wasn't leaving it behind.

"I don't believe in the afterlife." He was frightened, like a child.

"Noel, you have passed on. And yet you're here

talking to me. And there are angels here. Of course there is an afterlife! Your tie to this world has been broken. You liked routine, and the sameness of life. And that's what has you stuck here in Frances' house; the order, the routine, the safety of the physical. But you belong somewhere else now. Meet your family and your friends again. It's time to move on now."

He came. Reluctantly. It was difficult for him to leave the security of what he knew. He didn't want an adventure.

"I promise you that where you are going is bliss. Let's go."

He stood up straight. Case in hand. And he took his leave, over the bridge. Fear left him as he made his way over to the lights and his loved ones. He was overjoyed when he waved back – with his two arms. The little brown case on the ground.

I was back in my own shell in Frances' room, and the whole place reeked of disinfectant. I gave thanks for a job well done.

That day, I learned that a spirit can leave a body under stress, can leave while the body is still undoing its tie to this world.

Frances' house was quiet and still again. But I knew it wouldn't last.

+ + +

Three months later.

"Margaret, the knocking has started up again."

I knew immediately who it was.

"Hello, Frances."

"Knocking and banging all last night. A ferocious din. I know what you're going to say, but I can't do it. I need you to come."

"It's Paul."

"You what!? I don't believe you! He was buried yesterday."

"It was a tragic passing. He's telling me that he looked for help at his funeral – in the church, actually – and he found you."

"I didn't go to the graveyard."

"Neither did he. He left with you. He's in shock himself. He's showing me his heart; a faulty valve. He's sorry for annoying you, but he doesn't know what else to do. He wants me to say 'Sudden Death Syndrome'."

"He was found in his apartment. Sitting reading the newspaper. They're waiting for the results of the autopsy."

"He was separated from his wife. They have a young son."

"Yes."

"He is saying Teresa and Joseph and Margaret belonging to him have passed over."

"Yes. It's okay, Margaret, you can stop. I know it's him. Can you come up today? Please."

"Frances, it's time you did this yourself. You know this young man well. He has no bad intentions toward you. He is lost and has come to you for help. You are the beam. You know he won't be a difficult spirit to guide."

"I can't, Margaret. I'm not able for it. What if I can't help him? Please. Do this one. And I promise it'll be the last. I'll do it from now on."

I agreed. I knew she'd get her opportunity with another spirit soon enough.

That night, whilst lying awake in her bed, Frances told Paul that help was coming. That he would be going to his new home the following day.

I went up to the house the next afternoon and brought Paul over the bridge.

**+ + +**

A mere eight weeks later, the time came for Frances to develop her own gift.

"Margaret, there's someone in the house. The banging is off again, the lights going on and off. I know what you're going to say –"

"Frances, this is your time. Pauline needs your help."

"Pauline?!"

"Yes. She took her own life and she's looking for your help. She says that you know her."

"Yes. Yes, I do. I'm related to her husband. She committed suicide recently."

"She found your light, but she wants to go over to the next life. She can't find her way alone. Frances, you have nothing to fear. She is a kind spirit and you need to reach out to her. I'm not coming this time."

"Oh Jesus. What'll I do? What'll I do? I can't believe this. I need your help."

"Bless yourself. Ask your own guides to protect you. Ask for permission to help Pauline, that it be God's will that her trapped soul pass over to the kingdom of heaven. At the end, you must give thanks and ask to be protected as you come back down to your reality, your earthly life. Whatever you use is symbolic; candlelight is wonderful. Or some rosary beads, if you wish. Whatever you can focus on and protect yourself with. Go up to your room; this seems to be the centre of most of the activity."

"Oh Jesus. Oh God."

She was hyperventilating.

"You can't keep calling me. This is what you're supposed to be doing here, in this life. You will know what to do. This is your gift."

"Oh Jesus. Okay. Tell me. Tell me again. Okay. What do I do?"

"You know what you have to do. You have watched me in your house. We have talked it through many times. You have this gift. Put the phone down. While there is nobody home, gather your thoughts. Quieten your mind. Light a candle. Ask for protection so that nobody can harm you. Use your mind energy and find Pauline."

She gasped.

"You *will* find her. Then visualise both of you going to the bridge, and bring her to the top of it. You can't go any further."

"Oh fuck. I'm a nervous wreck. Can you not come and do it with me?"

"You are not a nervous wreck. You will see. You'll feel so calm doing it. This is your role. You can't keep passing it up. These souls are coming to you for help. And you are being shown what your potential in this life is."

"Jesus Christ."

"Put the phone down and take a deep breath. Call me when you are finished. This is a giant step for you. And for Pauline."

+ + +

Half an hour passed. The phone rang.

"I did it! I did it!"

She was ecstatic.

"I found her. I brought her to the bridge. I told her that there were people there waiting for her and that her family on earth would be well looked after, until they meet her again. And it worked. I knew the minute I saw her go that my house was clear again. I just have a *knowing*. I know it worked. I can't believe it! She turned back and waved me on, like you said she would."

She went on.

"And another great thing happened – I saw my dad. When I was taking Pauline to the bridge, I saw my dad rolling up his shirt sleeves, as if he was getting ready to do some work, to help me. I knew I didn't need to worry. That he would bring Pauline over, that he'd make sure she got home. And he did."

And so began the launch of Frances' new "career" and one less person calling on me.

+ + +

A young woman approached me when I was in a restaurant recently.

"Do you remember me? My name is Melissa."

"I'm sorry. I don't think I know you?"

"You're Margaret. You helped me when I was a little girl."

Suddenly I could see her curly little head.

"I do remember. How are you?"

"I never heard the sounds again. The wailing or the shouting. The noise of the wheels. And I never saw the boy on the bike after that day."

"I'm very glad."

She smiled.

"And my dad didn't see the man on the stairs again. Although he didn't go up the stairs in the dark ever again either."

She gave me a hug and walked away.

# NINE

## THE SOULLESS

I do believe in the existence of negative presences, the existence of evil manifestations. But these are not spirits, and they are not lost souls. They have no good within them, no saving graces. Such presences are soulless entities and they do wish to "haunt". Their desire is to incite fear and dread.

Evil feeds off fear, depression, arguments, wars. It can grow and it can take form if it is fed sufficiently. I have encountered evil on several occasions and am always overwhelmed by its power. Evil has to wait to be asked in, to spot a little crack in a person's aura, but then it will seize its opportunity and feed itself. As it grows, so does its power and its ability to cause damage. It can develop a "mind" of sorts, but it is always without a soul. The more people are suffering as a result of its foul deeds, the more power it feels. It knows no good and comes from an evil place.

It can be a frightening thing, but the wonderful news is that it can be dispersed and "recycled" into light energy. Just as we don't throw the weeds back into the field having pulled them up, it's not in our interests to dump this negativity back to its source. It needs to be diffused and the energy harnessed and converted for better.

+ + +

*"We moved into the cottage in October 2003. It was our dream home and about 360 years old. The first thing we noticed was that one corner of the sitting room, right beside the fire, was always cold. But because of the age of the cottage, we paid no heed to it.*

*"One evening on my way home from work, about half a mile from the cottage, I heard children's voices in the car. Like I was hearing a radio in the distance. I remember reaching for the radio to turn it off, only to discover it wasn't on at all. For about two weeks, half a mile from the cottage, I would hear the children's voices in the car.*

*"A month later, my partner and I were painting the sitting room late at night. My daughter was upstairs in her room asleep. There was music coming from upstairs. We listened and thought it unusual because it wasn't Connie's type of music. We went up and she*

*was still sleeping, no music from her room. We went into our bedroom and the music was coming from our stereo, which was unplugged.*

*"Over a short time, more and more strange things started to happen in the house; alarms going off, radios coming on, voices in the bedroom, cold areas in the house. We decided to make a Ouija board. It was that night we unwittingly issued an open invitation to more visitors, unwanted visitors.*

*"We took the board upstairs and asked if there was anyone present. We persisted for a while. The next night we did the same. The pointer on the board slowly moved itself to 'NO'. We didn't fall asleep that night. We were both still awake at four o'clock, tossing and turning and unable to breathe with the suffocating presence in the room. The following morning, we noticed a large water stain in the shape of a circle on the ceiling over the bed.*

*"Over the next week, we heard footsteps, doors shutting and opening, voices in the house. Nothing that could be explained in any logical way. We were completely unnerved. Things grew more and more sinister. We were watching a film in front of a roaring fire but the room was freezing cold, absolutely icy. The next day, there was white paint all over the stairs. My daughter was getting increasingly unsettled so I brought her to stay at her grandmother's house until we got the activity under control.*

*"Things became really horrible in the house. Doors opening and closing all night, loud voices in the*

hallway, knocking on the wall. We were barely sleeping at all now. One morning, Anne sat down in the kitchen and opened the seal on a new bottle of mineral water. She began pouring it into the glass. She turned around to put the bottle down and I stared at the glass in disbelief. There was black soot in the glass. I looked up to see if it had fallen from the ceiling – trying to be logical, though why would it have come from the ceiling? Anne grabbed the glass and threw it into the sink. We couldn't speak. The threatening atmosphere was taking over our lives. We then heard what sounded like an argument in the hall. We were able to distinguish a man's voice. We were both having palpitations. Thank God we experienced these things together or we'd have each thought we were going mad.

"Things went quiet for a couple of days. We were lulled into a false sense of security. We went to bed feeling a bit lighter about everything. Anne fell asleep immediately. I lay awake for a while in the dark and then closed my eyes. I hope I can explain this correctly; I wasn't actually asleep, but it felt like a dream. It felt like a dream because I had no control over stopping what happened next. I had an extremely violent, sexual 'dream', verging on the grotesque. I won't describe it in detail; the very thought of it still makes me shiver. I remember screaming 'NO' at the top of my voice but no sound coming out. My heart was racing afterwards. As I lay there, awake and terrified now, the mattress began to move underneath me in a wave-type motion. I conked out.

"Two nights later, the same thing happened, but in reverse. I fell into a deep sleep straight away and Anne had a sexually violent dream, and again, the mattress started moving in a wave-like motion underneath her.

"Everything felt out of control. We couldn't think straight; we were exhausted and we truly didn't know what to do. The happenings in the house were getting the better of us. We took the Ouija board outside and burned it.

"A couple of nights passed with the threatening presence still in our room, but we slept this night. We slept so deeply that we even slept through the alarm. I jumped into the shower and noticed as I dried my hair with a towel in front of the mirror that my nostrils were completely caked in soot. And my ears. Anne was the same. We went back into our room and we both felt a level of fear that, despite everything, we hadn't experienced before. This was dangerous. The velux window above the bed was completely black, on the inside. The walls by my side of the bed were completely black. Black with soot. Every bit. The front of the wardrobe was clean but inside – at the back – was completely black. The clothes in it were marked with soot, as though something had gotten in there and then left. The marks were very distinct, very black. There were black finger marks all over my side of the bed. We were dealing with something very real and very dangerous. There was no way anyone could say we were imagining things now.

"Another night, another awful and vivid 'dream'. I

dreamt that a little girl, about eleven or twelve years old, was taken from our house by a man and dragged by her ankles to the bottom of the garden, raped, killed and buried in a shallow grave that was full of muddy water. I woke up terrified. As I moved my legs in the bed, I noticed that the bottom of the bed was soaking. I don't mean wet; I mean soaking. From my knees down to the bottom of the bed. It was like someone had poured buckets of water onto the bed.

"After dinner the next day, the house became filled with an unbearable stench. It got stronger and stronger. A rotting, overpowering smell. We checked shoes, socks, pipes, bins, everything; looking for a logical explanation. There was none.

"In desperation, we decided to try to get a medium to come to the house and talk to the presence for us. I tried three names I found on the internet, but they wouldn't come. I remember sitting at my desk with tears falling down my face. I remembered my colleague Jennifer talking about a medium – her name was Margaret – that she had been to the year before. She had even given me her number although I don't know why, because I wouldn't ordinarily consider going to one. I found the number in my diary."

+ + +

I answered the phone one afternoon to a hysterical-sounding woman.

"Hello?"

"Is that Margaret?"

"Yes."

"Oh thank God. You've no idea how glad I am to speak to you."

"Can I help you?"

"Oh God. I hope so. My house is haunted." She went on, her voice full of panic. "I'm from Kells. And my house is haunted. There are terrible presences. We can't sleep. There's soot and water appearing from nowhere. Voices and noises and music. It's a cottage and it's 360 years old and . . ."

She went on detailing the horrors in the house. My head started to spin. I didn't like the sound of this at all. I liked gentle spirits, in my healing room, with messages for their loved ones. There was nothing benign about what this girl was describing.

But I knew I wasn't going to get away with hanging up, with not trying to help her out.

I heard myself ask: "Where's Kells?" I reached for a pen and paper with my free hand.

She was unable to stop herself now she had someone prepared to listen.

"We've rung other mediums but they wouldn't come. We've woken up to the whole room covered in black soot. On all the clothes in the wardrobe, our bed, our faces, inside our nostrils, everywhere. But there was no fire on. We're on the verge of insanity at this stage . . ."

*Jesus.*

I kept hearing the word "Evil" in my head. As she

spoke, I got a bad taste in my mouth – a strong, chemical taste as though I had been given an injection into my gums. I knew there was a bad energy in the house.

"We haven't slept. We're terrified. We can't afford to move house. We're at our wits' end. We tried to stay calm, to keep things normal, but now I've been out of work for the last six weeks because of it. I feel like I'm losing my mind. The other morning, the bottom of my bed and my legs were soaking. Soaking wet with muddy water. What's going on? You have to help us."

She was pleading, her voice full of terror. I wanted to help but wasn't sure that I could. Truth be told, the more she said, the more unattractive a proposition it was becoming.

"What's your name?"

"Gormla."

"Gormla, I don't really do this kind of thing so I don't want to give you false hope. Give me a couple of days to think about it."

✛ ✛ ✛

My son Steve went berserk when I got off the phone and told him what had happened.

"You are *not* to go down there. Absolutely not. You don't know what you're dealing with. You have to look after yourself. You are NOT to go. Please."

I asked my guides if evil would manifest in that way. I heard a clear Yes. Just as there is good, there can be evil and blackness. I asked for guidance from a higher level; would I be equipped to go down to these people and could I help them? I had no sooner finished asking the question than my mouth, my throat, my nose became filled with the overpowering and distinct smell and taste of bleach. I gagged. It felt like it was running right through me. I knew what I was to do. Bleach kills the unknown – bacteria, filth, dirt, germs. I had to go down there.

I phoned the girl back, took down directions and made an arrangement. We were meeting on Sunday afternoon in a car park in Kells. I told Steve I was having late lunch with friends.

+ + +

I had the usual fears that morning about my car holding up, about finding the place on time, about meeting strangers. Added to this was my anxiety about what I would find when I got there.

From the car park, they drove ahead of me to the house. It was a good thirty-minute journey. I smoked alone in my car, the whole way *begging* my guides and Michael the Archangel to protect me. And to get me out of the place alive. Passing by winding country roads en route, I have to admit that I did consider taking one of them – making a break for it and spending the afternoon anywhere else.

We pulled up outside the most idyllic, quaint little cottage. Beautiful. I relaxed.

I walked through the front door and thought I would vomit. The energy in the house was sickening, just sickening. The smell was intolerable; like sewage. And the cold was unreal. It was colder inside than out.

My face must have fallen because Gormla, who was watching me closely, immediately apologised for the cold and the smell.

"We can't explain it. The heat is on all of the time and the smell gets worse the more cleaning we do."

I was suddenly getting information from all sides, crowding in on me. About these girls, their pasts, vicious sexual abuse, the house itself. I started rattling off what was coming to me. I gave them the names of those in their lives who had passed on, loved ones who were there trying to protect them. I could see two other lovely, gentle spirits there also; not connected with the couple, but rather attached to the house. I relayed everything I heard. Then I was shown a Ouija board. I knew there was an evil presence here – not spirits of the type that I was used to dealing with.

"There are evil entities in this house. I can see that you have been using a Ouija board."

They said nothing, but nodded.

"Jesus Christ! At your age. You should know better. It's like prodding a raging bull. You don't know what you're dealing with. None of us do. You opened yourselves up and invited these things in. And because you both became so terrified, you gave this entity – this energy – strength. You gave it life. And energy to feed off. Every little thing that happened in the house, you were jumping, frightened, giving it more energy; feeding this weed. The more fear you felt, the more the darkness was growing. Where is the board now?"

"We burned it. Outside."

I sat and did readings for them both. I needed them to trust me. Before I could cleanse the house, rid it of the negativity and the power of the presence, I needed them to believe in me and be calm and comfortable. Their fear was the energy's greatest tool.

They showed me upstairs. In the bedroom, soot was caked all over the white duvet. One wall was entirely black. The strangest thing was the wardrobe. The clothes in the back of it were covered in soot, absolutely destroyed with it. The back wall of the wardrobe was totally black, filthy. But the front was clean.

This was a devious and conniving entity. And it was driving these women to the point of madness.

They showed me the other room, where the music would come on – blaring – in the middle of the night. They would have to jump up and turn it off. Every time, the plug for the CD player was on the floor while the music boomed around the room. On and off it went, although there was no power, no electricity getting to it.

The smell in parts of the house was more obnoxious than in others. I can't even describe it. It was foul, toxic. I could feel it going down my throat. The three of us coughed walking around the rooms. And the iciness, the bitter cold was simply unreal, even though the heat was on in every room. The air was dripping with malevolence.

The cottage itself was beautiful and I could see they had put a lot of love into decorating it. But, as it stood, nothing could have made someone stay in this house for more than two minutes.

I prayed every second I was there.

The horrific sexual abuse that they had both suffered as children kept being played in my mind. I could see that the evil energy that had been released into the house had fed on this over the last few weeks; it had somehow "re-enacted" these horrific rapes on them, picking up their weakest moments with which to torture them. I can't explain this at all, explain how this happened, but it did. This energy had pinned them down and they lay like lead and relived the horrors of their individual pasts. They confirmed everything I said.

I could see that this evil entity had some form of intelligence; by making itself part of these terrifying memories, it was feeding itself with their fear.

As we stood downstairs again in the kitchen, out of the corner of my eye I saw this shape come around the corner into the room. It came to stand around Gormla and I saw that Anne could see it too. Her face became filled with terror. She whispered: "Margaret, can you see it?"

"Yes. I see it."

It wasn't a man or a woman or a being; it was like a mass of insects moving together in harmony. The shape was changing. As I looked, it wrapped itself around Gormla, and went right down into the top of her head. I swear to God, on all of my children's lives, we watched it get thin in shape and then dart inside her, through the top of her head.

*In the name of all that's sacred!*

I jumped up. It was horrific. I grabbed Gormla. I pulled her head back. I've no idea why. Her face was changing, into ugliness. I put my hands on her head and tried to drag this entity out with all my mind energy, my physical strength, my prayers, my curses, anything I could muster. I had no fear; I was almost possessed myself. I could feel its energy cower; it started biting; my hands were scraped at.

"GET OUT OF THIS GIRL, in the name of Jesus Christ and in the name of everything that's Holy! GET OUT!"

It was mind-to-mind combat.

I fell backwards across the chair with its force as it screeched out of her body.

I put my hand on her head and I sealed it completely. I imagined a steel plate at the top of her head.

The spiritual centre at the top of her head, which should spiral outwards into the light and the universe, was spiralling inwards. Because she had been depressed for much of her life, her centre opened inwards and she attracted negative things inside her, right down. The more she was depressed and low, the more this funnel stretched down within her, which allowed this creature to just dart straight into her.

I held her and sealed her up.

*Please God hold the steel on her head. Please let her have some comfort. Please make that dirty, foul being be gone from her. I will open her a little again later, gently, so that she can heal herself.*

Anne was crouched down in the corner of the kitchen, crying. Otherwise, the room was quiet.

+ + +

Things had calmed down a bit and I had a chance to think. I realised that I didn't know whether to phone an ambulance, the police, or what I should do.

I heard myself say: "Listen girls, go and sit in the car. Leave me here alone for a while. I will wave down to you when I am finished. I need to cleanse this house."

I could see my breath as I spoke. The air in the kitchen was actually freezing. I shut the door behind them.

I can't do any of this personally. I have a "team" of sorts. I always see Michael the Archangel, wearing a soldier's uniform – what I would describe as a Roman soldier's uniform – and carrying a huge shield with a sword and serpent on it. And with him are my guides and, in this case, these girls' angels. I smelled the overpowering fumes of bleach again within me and I felt comforted.

The cleansing would begin. Even though the house was still icy, I was feeling warm now. These women brought in this entity, these ugly energies, and the team of good spirits would get rid of them. It was a battle. A battle of wills; good against evil. I had my rosary beads and my little crucifix to strengthen me. I cleansed every corner, every window, every floor board, every skylight; I left nothing to chance. I blessed everything. The rancid, damp, rotten smell started to lift.

The walls were still full of soot, despite the fact that they had been washed again and again and again. In the washing of the walls, a picture had emerged. A beautiful, angelic face on the wall. I took consolation from this, as I worked. I took out the sheets, the blankets, the clothes. Everything that had soot on it. Not once did I feel overwhelmed or inadequate. I felt completely empowered by the Holy Spirit. My mind energy and my aura were stretching out and I could feel I was well protected.

I was told to go and clap very loudly around the house. I went to every corner and clapped as loudly as I could. My hands were stinging. Eventually, I had done every door, every nook and cranny and every cubbyhole. I stood and asked for verification – a sign – that the job was done.

There was a *bang* on the roof outside the cottage. Like a clap of thunder. And then a second one. Louder. BANG. And then I heard the word "Dispersed".

I ran outside. I felt excited. I waved down to the girls.

"Come on! Come on in!"

They charged up the field.

I didn't mention the bangs. I never like to put thoughts into people's minds.

"What were those bangs!? The bangs on the roof?" I was thrilled.

"They were your proof. Your home is cleansed. Nothing sinister will find its way here again, unless you invite it in. You need to let go of your fears, your depression. You cannot feed these energies with negativity."

I gently did healing around both of these women. I could see the light around them now. The darkness was gone.

They led me back to the car park where we had met. They drove and I followed. I was very tired but I was equally happy. I had cleared a tiny little patch of evil that day and made room for new growth, positive growth.

+ + +

They phoned me a couple of weeks later, full of relief and cautious happiness. Their house seemed to be a safe place. They'd even had the confidence to invite friends around the night before.

And now, years later, they still check in with me from their warm, light-filled home.

# TEN

## THE LITTLE FLOWER

I liken being a medium to being a satellite dish. Vibrating at a different frequency, I can receive and project pictures and messages that can be understood by the sitter. Spirits have a higher vibration and frequency than humans. When they want to contact their loved ones, my vibration is raised to allow communication with them, thus allowing me to hear, see and feel the energy of people who have passed over.

I tried to go about this work quietly. I worried that if I didn't, it would be taken from me. I was becoming settled with it, accepting it as part of myself and taking comfort from it now. I had a new perspective on life, a new outlook on people. I felt privileged. The phone calls kept coming, now from all over the world. I wasn't complacent, but I was content. I didn't want to lose that feeling.

By now, I had learned to close myself down well after readings, not to leave myself open to messages and unwanted intrusion. This was a great achievement for me because, up until then, I felt I had no control. And it had been very draining to be open – working – all of the time. Now I could socialise a little again. And I could save my energy for when people came for readings or healing.

**+ + +**

A man came to see me. He was small in stature and wore a black suit. He had been driving for a few hours to get to me. He sat down.

A small, rotund lady appeared.

"Your mother, Kathleen, is here."

He blessed himself.

"Oh my God."

Kathleen gave him the names of his brothers and sisters, to put him at his ease. When he relaxed into the chair, I felt his mother's presence overshadow me. I was still getting used to this myself.

"Please watch me, watch what I'm doing. Your mother is making me do the things she used to do so that you'll recognise her. She was a rather wide lady."

I mimed sitting in a chair, cutting the top off a pair of tights with a scissors, until there were only two stockings left. I bent down and acted as though I was rolling up the individual stockings onto my legs, just as far as my knees. I then reached for two elastic bands to hold them up at the top. I rolled these bands up my legs, one at a time.

All the time, I talked her son through his mother's actions.

"Jesus Christ. That's exactly the way she did it. 'Tis her. 'Tis definitely her."

He was blessing himself again.

I sat back and smiled her smile.

We were both delighted. Marvellous.

Then there was a thud in the room, as something fell from thin air and landed on the carpeted floor between us. We jumped. Less sure of ourselves now.

We looked down. A worn brown sock lay on the ground at his feet. I don't know who got the bigger fright.

I felt I should fake some bravery and pick it up.

"Holy Mother of God." He blessed himself repeatedly. "That's my father's sock! I swear to God. It's the exact sock that he'd have worn."

I could feel Kathleen's shoulders shake and her laugh overtake me.

Her poor son was pale.

"Only I was here for it myself, I'd never believe it."

He read my mind.

I threw the sock. No thud. No noise at all. Logic was not going to explain this.

He was mopping his brow with a handkerchief.

I knew there had been no old brown sock in my room before he came. I told him to take it with him.

"I'm the hard man in the family. How am I going to

explain this to them all?" He pushed it into his pocket.
"You won't. Like I can't."

+ + +

A lot of men who come are often sceptical, reserved, embarrassed that they're here at all.

I opened my front door to see a man in his early forties chewing gum.

"Paul?"

He nodded. He had come for a reading. He strutted in and sat back in the chair, arms folded. Chewing. *Impress me.*

*Oh God. This is going to be bloody hard.*

"If you wouldn't mind unfolding your arms, because you're blocking off all the energy. Sorry, but I need you to relax and be a bit more open. You will get a lovely reading."

He moved as though he was going to get up to leave, but then sat back. Arms dangling now at his sides. Still chewing.

His mother's spirit came in. She identified herself and named the rest of their family. I didn't look at him. I tuned inward and did my best to disregard his derisive frown. I relayed everything I was seeing and hearing.

As the reading continued, I glanced over at him.

The chewing had stopped. The expression on his face had changed. He looked stunned. Not nearly as self-possessed as he had been on the step.

He didn't utter a word but he nodded when our eyes met.

"Paul, this is your mother speaking through me. I'm not trying to fool you."

I was impressed to sit beside him for a minute. The strongest scent of roses engulfed him. It was breathtaking. I didn't say anything. I was aware of the smell but I knew it wasn't for me. It was for him. I waited a moment and then I heard his voice for the first time.

"What is that smell? It's overpowering. The smell of flowers."

I was delighted he had smelled it.

"It's for you."

A mist appeared in front of us. The temperature dropped in the room. Dropped to iciness. I was watching the mist. A figure appeared as the mist faded. I spoke as I watched.

"I don't want to scare you, but I'm going to tell you exactly what I see as it happens. There is a lady – Oh! It's the Little Flower, it's Saint Theresa – standing in front of you. She has appeared out of the mist. She is smiling at you. She's carrying roses in her arms."

My heart was racing. I was in awe. She invited me to touch her garment. It was coarse – a coarse wool. I described her clothes to him, down to her shoes and creamy socks. She didn't dwell on me. She was there for Paul.

His eyes filled. He whispered, choking back the tears: "Nobody knows this, but I always pray to her.

She's my favourite saint."

"Well, her smile for you is beyond this world. I've never seen a smile like it in my life."

The apparition faded – although it was more than an apparition; she was real, standing there, as real as he was. The room's temperature returned. It was a magnificent experience and I was honoured to have been a part of it.

Paul was quietened and humbled by his miracle.

A few days later his wife phoned me.

"I'm amazed at my husband's belief, at the change in him since he went to see you. When he got home, he went straight into the children's bedroom – without a word – and took a picture of Saint Theresa down from their wall. He got a nail and the hammer out of the shed and hung the picture up over our bed."

+ + +

A girl in her early thirties came for a reading.

I was surprised when I opened the communication from the spirit world and a man entered immediately, saying: *I am her husband.*

She was so young to be a widow.

"Your husband is here."

He gave his name and how he had passed over. She became teary. He saw this, but wanted to lighten the moment. Immediately, he asked me to say: *Love the boobs.*

*Pardon?! I will not.*

He shouted it at me. *Go on: LOVE – THE – BOOBS.*

He was adamant.

I took a deep breath.

"I'm sorry. I'm embarrassed, and I hate saying this. I hope he's not going to go any further with it, but he wants me to say, 'Love the boobs.' Sorry. I hope you don't think I'm rude. He's quite insistent."

"Oh – My – God!" She blushed. She covered her face with her hands.

He said nothing for the minute. Laughing at her reaction. Watching her.

I waited. I hoped she wasn't offended.

Eventually she took her hands down from her face.

"You won't believe it but I'm just after having a boob job . . ."

The two of us – three of us – laughed.

"Does he know all about it? Oh God!"

"Well, obviously he does! I'm just relieved it's evidence he's giving you. I thought he was going to start talking about sexual things! I'd have had to cut him off!"

"Oh God, Margaret! They don't see everything that we do, do they!? Oh Jesus."

"They tend not to go into our personal lives. He wanted to impress you and also compliment you at the same time. He's thrilled with himself."

"He's the same little shit. Still managing to embarrass me, even when he's dead."

+ + +

I felt a spirit's energy enter the room as I waited for a client one day. It was male, quiet and shy.

The lady for the reading arrived.

I knew by the male presence waiting that it would be a slow reading. He gave me his name and then I could see him, wearing a tweed overcoat and a trilby hat. I described him, his face, his build, his clothing to her. He was smiling.

"That's my dad."

Then I got the most unmerciful pain in my leg. I nearly went into shock, it was so severe. I had to catch my breath and pull myself together to speak.

"Your father is impressing upon my body a very bad pain in his right leg. Dreadful. It was the cause of the problems that finally killed him."

"Yes."

I sat back on the couch, held my leg out and started to shake it, as though to shake the pain away, to release it.

"Oh God! That's just like him. That's what he did. Shake his right leg. Just like you're doing."

He brought me to a hospital bed, and I was him for a moment. I was being spoon-fed, and I really didn't like it. He didn't like it. I relayed this.

"He's appealing with his eyes for you, for the rest of your family to let him go. It was just too hard for him to stay here. He felt that he had no dignity. He couldn't bear being reduced to that state. He wanted to leave the physical world. He wanted to go, with gentleness, with ease."

This girl sobbed. Through her tears, she said, "That's exactly what happened. I know he's happier now."

"Yes, he is. Blissfully so. He says 'No more tears' for him."

+ + +

A garda phoned me. He introduced himself. He had heard I was a medium and hoped I could help. The gardaí were having trouble tracing the whereabouts of an elderly lady who had been missing for some time.

"We're prepared to try anything at this stage."

I was shocked that a policeman would call me for assistance. If I'm driving with a cigarette in my mouth and I see a guard, I nearly jump out of my skin. I throw it out the window. I don't know why. I start to panic about my tax, wonder if I'm speeding. I have a peculiar fear of the law. *Is he going to want to come here to talk to me?* I started looking around the kitchen for possible violations.

He was still talking into the phone when, clear as day, I could see the lady he spoke of.

I could see her house; two-storey, painted a yellow colour with brown windows. The door was centred between two windows. As she came down the path to open her little gate, she had a dog with her. She turned to the left, her left.

I relayed all of this.

"Don't go to the right, toward the canal. You're dragging the canal and she's not there. She went the other way."

Now he was shocked. Quietly: "We've been dragging the canal for two days."

"Well, stop. You're wasting your time. She's not in it."

I was able to tap into her mind. I could sense that she was confused. She had left the house with her dog to go to visit a neighbour, Mary. When she got to where she had thought she was going, the neighbour wasn't there. In fact, she didn't recognise the house. It wasn't like she remembered. She became disorientated and rambled on looking for a recognisable face or familiar house. She turned into a housing estate, but got totally lost. She became very tired. She kept walking for a long time until she came to an incline, with hedging on both sides. She made her way up this narrow incline. I could see through her eyes; see a field over the hedging. She tried to get through, to get off this narrow, winding pathway. She was anxious and confused. She lay down to rest, with the dog.

He was listening intently on the end of the line.

"You will find her soon. She is disorientated."

"If you're tapping into her thoughts, communicating with her spirit, does that mean she's dead?"

"I'm not sure that I can answer that. I'm not always entirely sure what I can do. But I feel she's still alive."

I got a phone call that afternoon. They had found her in the field. She was alive, sleeping, with a touch of hypothermia. Her son confirmed that she had been diagnosed with Alzheimer's some time before.

+ + +

I forgot all about that episode, but I should have known I would draw upon it at a later date. That I would be called to speak for someone living with Alzheimer's. The spirits always prepared me in advance for what was coming down the tracks to me.

One day, months later, a woman named Carol came for a reading. I saw her father standing behind her; clear-skinned with thinning grey hair and glasses, but not elderly. Middle-aged.

I relayed this.

"I have two fathers. The one you've described is still living, but he has Alzheimer's."

"Your biological father is in the spirit world, standing with your mother. She says she passed on when you were a very young child."

She nodded. Tears running down her cheeks.

Her biological parents spoke to her for some time. But, all the while, this man was pulling me back, pulling at me for attention.

"This other gentleman – your dad – who is living, is pulling at me. He wants me to talk to you for him. He's afraid I'm going to neglect him."

"Can he talk to you? He's still alive."

"Yes, he can. It's mind-to-mind contact."

And with that, my stomach swelled up to the size of a football. He was giving me his physical pain, cramping and stretching. He gave me his name and the names of the nurses who were caring for him. He was particularly forceful about one nurse in particular whom he wasn't at all fond of.

"He has bad cramps, stomach pain. Swelling. He's showing me his colon. He has a sore eye and a short, persistent cough."

"Yes!"

She was taken aback.

"He wants me to tell you that he knows you go to see him all the time. That it's you who brings the flowers, tidies up the place, brushes his hair. He's very content and he does have the occasional lucid moment. He knows you are there and appreciates you treating him as though he is still fully alive, mentally and emotionally. He loves when you chat to him; he takes it all in. The best day he ever lived was the day he married the woman you call 'mum'."

He told his daughter exactly when he would pass over and how she would know, know in advance that it was coming. He knew that she needed to know, to have some idea of a time-frame. Things had been dragging on for so long.

"Nobody can imagine what it's like to go in every day, thinking he doesn't know me, knowing he'll never get well."

She was so relieved.

"He has his finger up now and he's saying you're not to cry when you're in there with him. You are to cherish those moments before he is gone to the next life."

"I will, Dad. I promise."

His spirit, his subconscious mind, was outside his ageing body, talking to his daughter to allow her cope with his current state and his imminent passing.

Carol was a far more calm, peaceful and accepting woman after their conversation.

# ELEVEN

## RELUCTANT SPIRITS

At this time of my life, my daughter Shauna had married and moved away. I mourned Shauna's loss from the home, but what she brought into the family a short time later was an amazing bundle of love, her daughter Molly, whom I adore. In the same year, my son Steve married and settled with his wife in Canada. I grieved his loss too, but I was grateful to God for letting me hold them both for so long. Within a year, Steve had a beautiful blond baby boy named Tate. My son Glen had moved to Cavan so he was no longer home in the evenings with me. I missed his company dreadfully. The house had emptied in a very short space of time. Nothing could have prepared me for the emptiness that their leaving brought.

But I tried to see that everything is progress, tried to

focus on the fact that I now had more time to think and to meditate. More space, more quiet. My abilities were developing. The nuances within readings were becoming more apparent to me. My ability to connect quickly and powerfully with spirits, to relay profound messages, was improving every day.

I had no clock in my healing room. I was unaware of the time. How long or short a time a reading lasted was not up to me; I had come to know that the spirits would take as long as they needed to communicate their messages. Some spirits were quick and easy and very willing to chat, whilst others were less so. To this day, I have never asked a sitter who it is they're hoping to hear from. I learned in the earliest days that the spirits who are needed most will come through.

In the majority of cases, spirits come through immediately; they are eager to give evidence, to confirm their identity, to give comfort and reassurance to the sitter. But not always. Around this time in the stillness of my home, I came to realise that within some of the readings I was doing of late, there were individuals who were not talkative at all, or who didn't come through as quickly, or who seemed to need time to work up to what they wanted to say.

Some readings lingered in my mind, ones where the spirit was less forthcoming, took longer, remained quieter. I wondered if I was to blame – did I not open myself up enough? During these readings I felt as though I was at a play where the curtains had opened and the stage was empty. That there, to the side, out of the corner of my eye, I could see the lead actor hiding in the wings – allowing himself to be seen, but nervous about taking centre stage and apologetic about delivering his lines. I found myself approaching the curtain and coaxing him on with reassurances, with promises of a friendly audience and guarantees of a good review.

And even so, the performance would remain disjointed and uneven, as though the lead was preoccupied and troubled. While he might eventually come to the centre stage, it would always be slightly to the back, shy – never up to the front, never actually getting close. Never touching the sitter, never stroking their hair or holding their hand. Hesitant about giving fully of themselves and yet hoping – more than anything – to be loved.

Over time I saw that it had nothing to do with me; that these spirits were actually uncomfortable about coming forward, that the issues or the healing to be given related to sensitive, thorny events and – as in life – were difficult to talk about. It took a lot of my energy to encourage them to come through. It didn't make sense to me at the beginning; I couldn't get to grips with these silent apparitions, with the coaxing and the urging that I would have to engage in to get them to speak.

I learned that the most reluctant spirits were those who had come to apologise to the sitter for hurting them in this life. Sometimes this hurt would have been abuse of a kind or sometimes it would have been that the spirits had passed over as a result of taking their own lives.

These were profound readings. The spirits came hoping for forgiveness but fearing rejection, judgement, anger. At the time, these were very difficult, emotional readings for me. And, as it seemed my ability was developing, there were more and more of them.

With time, I started to recognise them from the outset; I would sense the feeling of reluctance in the spirit world as soon as I began to tune in. I had left behind the anxiety that it was my doing, my fault. I accepted that this was to be the nature of certain readings and was the result of circumstances during the spirits' lifetime in this world. I was just the go-between. I reminded myself that I am not important in the readings; I merely give the spirits a voice. I am only the channel for these miracles. They're not mine.

Once I got an inkling that a reading was going to be of this nature, I was prepared for a long stay. It had to be gentle and slow for both people; it was like 1,000 counselling sessions all at once. Time to feel feelings. I think these readings are marvellous, as healing takes place for both the spirit and the living person. Maybe not at that moment, but eventually. At least the first step has been taken. It would often be the case that this would be the first time that an abuse had ever been aired, ever admitted, ever touched on, ever spoken of at all.

Far from angels with wings light and carefree, many

spirits who have inflicted pain – certainly those that I have encountered – are burdened by their actions in the next life and need to feel forgiveness to move on. The guilt remains when they pass over, and many will bravely take an opportunity to come through to apologise. I have been very privileged and humbled to have been part of these awe-inspiring readings and thank God that they have made life a bit easier for the people who came to see me on those difficult days.

*The following stories are of the most private nature, so I am including only the short excerpts that the individuals and families wish me to make known here.*

+ + +

A very handsome, immaculately dressed man came to the door for a reading. He smiled and extended his hand, but said nothing.

Even at this stage, I was still a little unsettled about doing readings for men. I worried about the all-too-common scepticism. I disliked feeling that I was to prove myself to them to prevent them scoffing, to allow them to justify their decision to come to see me at all.

But I read none of that cynicism on this man's face. He was shy and mild-mannered. I had no idea why he was here.

I was immediately told to sit beside him and hold his hand to give him support. I baulked a bit at this, but complied with the spirit's wishes.

"I hope you don't think me forward, but I have been told to hold your hand."

I became aware that something quite profound was about to take place. I didn't look at him, but turned my thoughts inward. I saw a lovely lady for an instant – his mother – but then I couldn't see her, although I could still feel her presence. I could feel her energy and I knew this was going to be important, and difficult. She was quiet, shy about speaking.

"Your mother Jane is here . . ."

Tears began to run down his beautiful face. He nodded for me to go on.

She allowed me to see her again. She wore a hesitant, timid expression. She started to speak. Her voice was a whisper.

"Michael, your mother says that you suffer with depression and that you have for a very long time. She knows you now, although she is not living here. You have a good life and a lovely family. She is very upset that you are so troubled."

She gave me her mannerisms and I took on her nervous voice and her gentle, compassionate tone. I relayed her evidence to him, softly, as she guided me – the names of his siblings, his address, where he lived with her as a child.

And then suddenly, I took a deep breath and words spilled from me – now louder than before: "It's alright, my darling Mick. I know what happened when you were six years old. You were sexually abused and I never knew about it. But I know now."

I paused to check that Michael wanted me to continue.

He sensed my question and nodded, his head down, eyes looking at his shoes. Tears hit the floor.

She gave me her words, her voice.

"Please don't think that I was ever ashamed or upset with you. You were only a little nipper. I take full responsibility for not knowing, for not helping and for the ignorance of the time we lived in." Jane was crying too. Pleading now: "My son, you were not at fault. I beg your forgiveness for not knowing then. You were a beautiful child. I am begging you to stop blaming yourself. I implore you, please don't allow it to ruin your whole life. I adore you and want you to live, to be happy. Don't hide away any more. Be proud of who you are and enjoy life's gifts. You are a wonderful son. Nothing was ever your fault."

He was shaking his head. He never looked up.

And then out of the silence, I heard this man speak for the first time.

"I can't believe it. I have never told a soul; I never dared to. And my mother knows."

"She has come to take the burden from you. She says you are not to be ashamed to look to her, to talk to her. She walks with you every minute of the day."

Michael's mother spoke to him for a very long time, about his depression, his debilitating existence, his low self-esteem. She gave him little thoughts to hold in his head, things she said when she lived here with him, to give him comfort and help him to heal.

+ + +

Kay arrived a few days later. She seemed nervous.

In an instant, I had the familiar feeling that hers was going to be a very profound reading. I was impressed to take her hand immediately. As soon as I did, the atmosphere changed and a peculiar stillness came over the room.

A very dim figure of a man slowly started to appear. It took a very long time for him to manifest. I had to give him my full attention and narrow my eyes to make out his outline. He didn't speak. He stood back, and yet he wanted to be there. I described to Kay how he was dressed and how he stood – humbly, with his head bowed. It was as though he felt he hadn't the right to be there.

I asked him to identify himself. I knew that he had hurt Kay deeply and was ashamed even to look at her.

In a low whisper, I heard "William".

"Kay, William is here."

A sharp intake of breath and her eyes narrowed. She looked at the floor.

"Do you want me to go on?"

She looked unsure. She started to sob.

"He says he is looking for your forgiveness. That is between you and him. You can choose not to hear him out. I will stop if it is too upsetting for you."

Silence.

And then a barely audible: "He ruined my life."

She was crying now, her shoulders hunched over. It was hard for me to maintain focus on William but I wanted to keep the sacred space open, to encourage him to stay, until she decided whether or not to listen to him.

"He is guilty of abusing you very badly, for which he is suffering too."

I could sense that William was making a real effort to apologise but he was full of shame and fear.

"He is trying to apologise. It is your choice to forgive him or not; he must live on with the consequences of his actions."

He was still standing in the shadows, when another spirit came forward. A very different energy was present in the room; Kay's mother Mary identified herself. Mary stood in front of William, less ashamed and less uncomfortable, but hesitant even so.

"Your mother Mary has come in. She is sorry."

No hesitation from Kay this time as she looked up, her voice raised: "How could she not have helped me? How could she have let this go on? I grew up feeling dirty and ashamed, believing that I wasn't good enough."

To ensure that Kay knew it was her mother, as Mary is quite a common name, her mother brought me to the farm they lived on and the family home. It was very isolated. I relayed the details of the home and the farm to her daughter.

Kay's voice got louder as she addressed her mother directly: "I needed you – I needed my mammy. Where were you then? How could you not have known? Not seen my sadness?"

Nothing in my own life could have prepared me for what was to happen in the next minutes. I found myself as a young girl – aged four – in a smelly shed on a farm. The stench of animals, of faeces was overpowering. I was shaking and frightened. All of a sudden, I was thrown on to the ground and the light vanished. A heavy man crushed me with his body weight. I took on the child's feelings; the terror, the sheer terror, the confusion. In the awful darkness.

*Jesus Christ.*

As this was happening, I had to describe it all to Kay. It was her experience, her healing. But I struggled. At times, the smell and the weight and the fear consumed me and I couldn't get words out. My stomach was churning, my legs pinned down. The odour from the man was obnoxious. I was Kay for those moments. But she didn't do this to me; it came from the spirit world.

A horrific rape took place.

And then, I was no longer the little Kay. Now I could see her. In her wellington boots, pulling down her dress, pushing her hair away from her face, standing tall, walking to the house. My heart went out to this child and I cried watching her tiny frame feigning bravery and taking steps through the pain.

Kay and I sat in silence for a moment, both of us lost in the aftershock of what had just occurred.

"That was me. My red wellies."

Something happened then that was another first for me. I was instructed to take a pen and write the words I was about to hear. As I wrote, I was to speak them aloud also:

*"Look at this child who has suffered and notice the straight back she has. And the strength she possesses, and her will to survive. This is your child and in your mind you must go back, take her from that shed, and embrace her. It may be difficult for you, but in order that your life progress in a different way, this is what you must do. Tell this child that no-one will ever harm her again, as you are the adult now and you are her Protector. You will merge with your loss of innocence and you will draw from her strength. If you hold her to your heart, Kay, she will make you whole again."*

At last, a little smile from Kay through the tears.

"I feel a bit excited, Margaret. I can see that little girl. I want to make it better for her, for me."

I was humbled by her strength.

"You know, I thought I would get sick when he came in at the start. I was going to leave. But I'm glad I stayed. I need to get beyond this. And I suppose I don't need him to suffer on and on either."

Kay was not being advised to dismiss the sin against her but rather to heal the child who was not at fault, to heal herself. Not to continue to feed the pain. She took the words the spirits had spoken home with her.

We can play a video of awful events over and over again in our minds and continue to hurt ourselves. But this is never the way forward.

+ + +

Last year, a grieving mother – Christine – came to my home.

"*I went to see Margaret because I wanted to contact my daughter, who had died a short time before. I wanted peace of mind, to understand why she left this life so early. I was nervous and apprehensive. I had been given Margaret's name and she came highly recommended by a friend, so I felt safe. Safe and yet nervous. I sat down and felt wounded, fearful, upset – all of the various feelings that comprise grief. Margaret knew nothing about me at all. Nor who had given me her number. She didn't ask me a single question about why I was there, where I was from, or otherwise.*

"*Straight away she said there was a young female energy coming through and she was coming with her head bowed. It wasn't that she didn't want to come but that she felt ashamed. She gave me my daughter's name – Amy – and said my little girl had been waiting for me.*

"*I felt relieved and more comfortable then. I knew this was my daughter and I understood why she was feeling sorry. She had taken her own life and left so much sorrow behind.*

"*Margaret's face changed. My daughter gave me the names of my other children – her sisters and brother – and also her father and her boyfriend. Margaret explained that this was proof for me to believe in her. My daughter then gave me the name Mikey. I knew who this was but I didn't say anything. I was to receive a letter in the post from him the very next day. My daughter also mentioned a photo, which Margaret described to me. She told me that she had been saving her spare money and that it was hidden in the back of this frame, behind the picture.*

*"Amy explained that she had been trying to give up drugs but that she was being bullied. A man of her acquaintance had tried to stab her. Some of the crowd she moved in were threatening her and forcing her to stay in the circle. She talked about these people and the dreadful accommodation they lived in. Margaret said Amy had ulcers on her legs and rolled around in bed with the pain of them. She showed Margaret prison bars and explained that she had had a hard life. She spoke about the abuse she suffered.*

*"Amy said she had been looking forward to going away – she had a trip planned to a sheltered house in Italy, where she intended to get clean. She had been saving for this, in her less dark moments when she could still make plans. She spoke about the angel that I had put on her grave. She remembered her two grannies and her uncle Joe.*

*"Everything Margaret said was absolutely true.*

*"I told Margaret that I wanted to know what had happened to Amy on that last night. Margaret's eyes closed. She described the room to me exactly, the room where my daughter had died. She could feel Amy's isolation and her desperation. She told me that she had taken sleeping tablets and then overdosed with hard*

drugs and alcohol. She could see her body lying on the bed in her locked room. I asked her to tell me where the syringe was found. And she did. It wasn't in her arm or her leg; it was somewhere else. Nobody had known this. Only the girl who had found her, and me.

"Amy told me that she is happy now. That she doesn't want to come back here, to this life. She says she is a guardian angel for her sisters and her brother. She told me to ask her father not to be so angry, to let go of the fury he feels over her death.

"When I got home he was waiting for me. He had emptied out the box full of Amy's things and found her diary while I was gone. He had been reading it and everything that she had just told Margaret about the bullying, the drugs, the stabbing, the intended trip to Italy and her deep sadness was there.

"Speaking to Amy that night has helped my husband and I to understand more fully what was going on in her life, the pain she was in, and how down she had become. He is calmer now. I have changed completely. I can't believe the effect that the reading has had on me. It has helped me enormously. It helped to lighten the pain and the weight on my heart. I feel less guilt about what we could have done, what we could have said. To hear her true feelings, her fear and her isolation, was very difficult, but things make more sense now. The cocktail of drugs and alcohol that she had deliberately taken had brought her to the next life.

"Since I went to Margaret, we speak more openly about Amy at home. About her life, our memories of *her, how we miss her. I was so upset and angry with her before; I couldn't believe that she would inflict this pain on us all. We all felt that way. But now we understand the pain that she felt, the helplessness, the fear, the sorrow she lived with every minute, her state of mind. It makes sense to us now. We are coping better as a family. And we are happy that she is happier. I know that I will be with her again in the future, in a better life."*

**+ + +**

People who have taken their own lives are not always reluctant to come through. Sometimes they are healing in the next world and are developing in ways that they never did during their lives here.

A girl came to me. Her uncle from the spirit world was in the room immediately. He was a fisherman. I could see him in a boat; I could smell the wonderful smells – the tackle, the fish, the salt, the oilskins.

She nodded in recognition.

It was quite a sad reading in many senses, as this man had taken his own life.

He gave her the name of his twin brother and then of his other siblings. He spoke about his son and how he was still connected to him. He wanted to reassure her that he wasn't in hell now, or in a purgatory or somewhere punitive. He knew that she worried about this.

She nodded, tears streaming down her face now.

I got constriction in my throat; I found it difficult to breathe. I knew that he was showing me how he had ended his time here. He had hanged himself.

He said that he was receiving great healing in the next life and finally getting a chance to pull himself together. This was something that he couldn't do in this world as he felt his life had become too troublesome for him. He thought that suicide was his only way out.

She nodded and said, "I understand." To both of us.

# Twelve

## My Miracles

Given all the publicity they're attracting in recent years, you'd be forgiven for thinking Angels were discovered in the last decade! The truth is, of course, that they've been shadowing us since the beginning of time. They have looked after me all my life, and I'd never have got to 62 if it weren't for them.

What is a miracle? A cure? The birth of a child? When pieces fall into place easily, like a perfect jigsaw? I can only talk about my own miracles.

My biggest miracle is that I woke up to my true calling in life before it was too late. I have had many accidents, obstacles and illnesses, but I rose up, or rather I was held up, and survived every time – against medical odds. The times of illness were also times for me to rest, to think, to absorb, to meditate and so gather wisdom and develop. When the illness passed and I was up and running again, my path seemed to have been cleared and laid out, lit up even, for me. My choices seemed obvious and simple. The phone would ring again and I would be guided to those whom I could help.

My own childhood wasn't without incident. Nor without its miracles. When I was two years old, I fell out of my father's car when it was turning around a bend at Chapelizod. I fell to the ground and hit my head off the tram tracks. When I was eight and on holidays with my family in Toomevara, I had a bad fall from a bicycle. The bike was speeding down a hill, out of control, past a church. Despite my intense fear, I just couldn't pass the church without showing the appropriate respect and I took my right hand off the handlebars to bless myself! I went over the handlebars and almost embedded myself in the road. I had severe concussion and was hospitalised. I've no memory of the next ten days, but no feeling of pain either. It seemed like stones were being picked out of my face for weeks.

At ten, I was in a very serious car crash with my family and our new baby sister Veronica. The car turned over a number of times. I was flung from the car and was lying on the main road. The car was unrecognisable. How half a dozen of us weren't killed, I don't know. We were all being taken care of that day.

I lurched along through childhood, one dangerous situation after another. Lots of opportunity for prayer.

And one miracle after another.

I was rescued from a burning house at fourteen. A couple of years later, I was assaulted while walking home to my house. As I lay on the ground with this man's knee on my stomach and his pungent breath on my face, feeling my clothes being torn, I was sure I was going to die:

*"Oh Angel of God, My Guardian Dear*
*To whom God's love commits me here*
*Ever this day be at my side*
*To light and guard, to rule and guide, Amen."*

And then I got away. Where I got the presence of mind to strike him in the head with my stiletto heel, I don't know.

There followed a horrific bus crash in Spain, and then being the only customer in a newsagents in the city centre when it was held up by an armed gang. I watched, with a gun stuffed in my mouth, while the shop assistant was held by the throat and beaten with the back of a rifle.

There followed a total hysterectomy, several cardiac surgeries, and a partridge in a pear tree.

+ + +

In June 1999, out of the blue, I had a very spiritual experience. I have a cardiac condition – a prolapse mitral valve – and have had many cardiac procedures and operations over the years. A routine visit was in order. While I was there, because of my age, my doctor examined my breasts and found a lump. He sent me for a mammogram.

"Margaret, something has shown up on your left breast. I need to do further tests to see how deep it is and ascertain what the best procedure is for dealing with it. We don't have time to hang about on this."

He kept talking, with his hand on my hand.

I never asked a question. Never said a thing.

He made an appointment for two days later.

I was terrified. Sick to my stomach. I spent most of the next 48 hours in my healing room, meditating and praying for healing energies. I sought guidance and spiritual help from above. I spent hours talking to my angels and visualising the lump dissolving, dissolving, dissolving, until it was non-existent. I heard a loud voice: "There is absolutely nothing wrong with you, Margaret."

I went to the hospital. Praying, my heart in my mouth. From the recent scan, they knew where the lump was and were doing exploratory tests. They did the first tests, and there was some toing and froing. They did more to confirm the results.

The results showed that the lump was gone. The doctor was dumbfounded.

"There is no sign of a lump, a cyst, a hardening, nothing. I can't explain it."

And then, the words I had heard the night before: "There is absolutely nothing wrong with you, Margaret."

It was a heavenly intervention for me.

+ + +

On the 13th of November 2006, I was out for dinner at my daughter's house when I became very nauseous at the table. I had pain on one side. The feeling continued for days, so I went to my doctor.

He said I had a cyst on my ovaries.

"Pardon!? I had a total hysterectomy twenty years ago. I have no ovaries. I don't even have my gall bladder."

"Well, there's a cyst attaching to something, and it's big."

The next day, I had numerous scans at the Charter Clinic in Dublin. I knew there was a problem when they asked me if I had a mobile number for my doctor. And the doctor's face was a giveaway. But in my wildest dreams, I never would have guessed what was ahead of me. It transpired that I had a very large ovarian cyst and we would "hope for the best". Those last four words sent me into a panic. Although surely there was a mistake. "I don't have any ovaries, tubes, womb, nothing."

I got an appointment the following day with the consultant gynaecologist who had done my surgery twenty years previously. It turned out that I had been left with a small amount of ovary to avoid my going into a full menopause at such a young age. I was admitted to Tallaght hospital immediately. It was seven o'clock on a Friday evening, but still all rush, rush,

rush. I was put into a taxi to the Beacon Clinic for MRI scans and tests.

On the Monday my consultant arrived, looking very concerned; I would venture that he was teary-eyed.

"I don't want to frighten you but there are a few problems, more than we had anticipated. I can only deal with one problem; the one at your ovary. What you have isn't a tumour, it's a mass. It has spread. We just don't know . . . we don't know, until we open you up. We don't know what we can do for you or what this will entail."

I didn't know where this was going. It wasn't a cyst, it wasn't a tumour. This was a mass. I started to see it in my mind's eye, and it didn't look good. He came to my bedside and took my hand.

"Listen, I'm going to operate on you over the next couple of days and have a look at this mass. But unfortunately, that's just the first part of things. You have other problems that have shown up. Your bile duct – up, under your rib cage, to do with your pancreas – your bile duct is very enlarged. But I can only talk about my end of things. We are going to do lots of blood tests. Have you lost weight?"

I felt there was a diagnosis hanging in the air that nobody dared put a name on.

"What can I expect?"

"Another surgeon is going to come to see you. He is a pancreatic oncologist. Someone who deals specifically with the bile duct. He will be in to see you in the morning and to decide whether or not he will operate immediately – the same day as I do – or leave you to recover from my surgery and then do his. We will decide between us what is best for you."

I was devastated. It transpired that there were two possible scenarios; the mass had grown so large that it was pushing up, pushing against the bile duct; or I had a very large tumour and also had pancreatic cancer. One was as bad as the next. I saw the oncologist. It was very clear that I was seriously ill. He had a sad look in his eyes. He opted to do his surgery the same day as the gynaecologist. He explained the reasons why he was pretty sure I had pancreatic cancer.

I had two name tags on my arm as I had two specialists. Twice as many problems.

I asked both doctors to draw a picture of what was going on inside me; with my stomach, my fraction of ovary, my pancreas. I needed to know; I needed to be able to visualise what I was dealing with.

I retreated into solitude, into a cocoon of prayer and peace. I've never experienced tranquillity like it. Ever. I don't know what came over me. I didn't phone anyone. I refused to feed this mass with negativity. Sometimes, people in your life who get bad news about you can – very unintentionally – harm you by creating negativity – "She looked terrible"; "I knew someone with that, and they only lasted six weeks." That kind of well-meaning Irish pessimism.

I retreated into my cocoon. There were angels all around me. That night was the most magnificent experience I have ever had. I kept thinking, "I am happy. I will be well. This can be healed." I was full of positive affirmations and a feeling of great peace.

The nauseous feeling had left me by now. I hadn't had it in a couple of days.

I spent my time visualising the mass, where it had started, where it had spread. I asked Jesus for special healing and to tell me how I could help. I immediately started to see small little round faces coming down through the opening in my head into my body. I asked them – this sounds crazy, but I asked them, these little faces with their little mouths – if they would please loosen this tumour away from the pelvic wall and from all of my vital organs; from my bowel, my liver, my stomach. I visualised it all.

I did that exercise all through my body, about ten times a day; I imagined these hard-working spheres carrying the bad cells up through my head and spitting them into a wheelie bin. Up and down, up and down through my body. I imagined the bin being dragged away to another world, changed into something positive. I went to sleep doing it, I woke up doing it. I trusted that, as it was what I had been shown to do, it was just what I needed to heal myself. It was as though I was having a spiritual operation, day and night. My "real" operation kept being moved and put off due to the changes taking place in my bile duct. St Joseph was always with me, speaking to me in the way that a father would, talking me through these days of waiting and healing. Even when I stood outside in the November weather, smoking.

I felt confident, well looked-after, very loved. I had

surrendered to whatever was God's will and yet I just knew it would all be fine. I was coming up to my second week in hospital. I was being scanned and tested every other day. My gynaecologist was still waiting, worrying. Looking to the oncologist to get the go-ahead for surgery.

The oncologist came in the following morning. He took both my hands.

"Margaret," he paused, looking for the words. I started to pray to myself. "I don't need to operate on you. I don't need to do anything at all. Your most recent tests are utterly clear. I can't explain how this can be. I apologise for putting you through everything. From your initial scans and MRIs, I was sure you had pancreatic cancer. That you were in big trouble. But now, there is nothing. No trace. I can't explain it. Well done. I'm going to leave you in the hands of your gynaecologist now. Goodbye."

Thank you, Jesus.

+ + +

The gynaecologist came in behind him, to steal this new sunshine.

"Margaret, I am going to operate on you tomorrow. The wait is over. I'll get in there and have a look at this mass. It will be a long operation, but you have been well prepared. Then I'll be able to give you my informed opinion on what to do next." He wore a very grave expression.

I was excited that night. Excited about my healthy pancreas, my healthy bile duct. Excited that this mass was going to be looked at, cleared out of me, taken away. I gave no energy to what it might contain, what it might suggest, what treatment I might need afterwards . . . It was on the way out.

I visualised the surgeon saying, "Margaret, it's all over. It's gone. It was nothing sinister." If I visualised this once, I visualised it a thousand times.

I was alone that night but I had plenty of company; there were angels and spirits all around me, full of smiles and encouragement. I knew it was going to be two out of two.

The next morning I trusted that God would guide my doctor's hands.

I woke up in Intensive Care.

As soon as I was with it, I was doing my own healing on the wound itself.

My consultant arrived.

"Margaret, what we removed from you was enormous. The mass was just huge. I haven't seen anything as big. The initial tests show no cancer. I had a good root around while I was in there, and everything is at it should be. I'm so delighted. I really did expect something different. Well done."

One of his surgical team sat with me for a few more minutes. "You know, Margaret, I've never seen anything like it. And yet it only took fifteen minutes for the mass to be entirely removed. It was the strangest thing. When you were opened up, the mass came away immediately. It was totally dislodged, unstuck to any organ, anything. Just sitting there. It came away straight into his hands. Honestly, I've never seen anything like it."

+ + +

The day after, I got out of bed and got dressed. I wanted to take a walk down the corridor. Each step I took I thought, "Gosh, I'm nearer the door. I'm closer to complete healing." I was excited. I asked to have the morphine stopped. I wanted to feel the pain; it was the feeling of healing. I would get a perverse pleasure from coping with it, managing it myself. I did my own healing; healing around the wound, healing of my body.

I walked the full length of the corridor on the fourth day. It filled with angels and spirits. All of them clapping and smiling. The applause was deafening. I cried and cried with joy for their encouragement. They were acknowledging the miracle, acknowledging my belief. I felt very privileged. I'll never forget that image. And no, it wasn't my imagination.

I went outside and had a celebratory cigarette. I knew they wouldn't deny me the one.

My wound healed very well and my stitches came out. I had quite a bit of pain, but I didn't mind it. It was the pain of healing. The pain of the road home. In a way, it was exhilarating to feel it.

I went home on the sixth day. I'd have run out the door if I could have, before they changed their minds.

It was December now and the Christmas lights were up. I felt more alive than ever.

+ + +

Six weeks later I went back to my gynaecologist. He hugged me when I came through the door. His happiness and relief were genuine.

"We have done every test possible on that huge mass and there isn't one single cancerous cell in it. To think that you will walk out of here today with a clean bill of health after what I saw on your scans a matter of weeks ago is just amazing." He shrugged his shoulders. "It's a miracle, Margaret."

That's exactly what it was.

+ + +

I was full of gratitude and happiness to be still on this earth. Three months later, with renewed enthusiasm for life, I travelled to Vietnam to visit an orphanage that had been set up by a European charity. While I was sitting downstairs in the lobby one afternoon, in the part of the building that was home to the children who were very ill, I heard a commotion. There was a bus outside. There were children being brought in and out, the wonderful nurses and staff members carrying the little mites to various rooms.

"Could you hold this baby, please?" A little girl was thrust into my arms.

"What's her name?" I asked as I received the bundle.
"Anna."

I was worried about hurting Anna, holding her the wrong way. She looked well, but I knew she had to be in very poor health. "Is she unwell?"

"She has a brain tumour."

I sat down and held her to me. I was left with her for a long time. She never took her eyes off my eyes. I was ready to sing "Anna Banana", but this child was well beyond that. There was a profound connection between us. She was an angel. I'll take the image of her face to my grave. I fell in love with her, in a matter of minutes. I wanted everything for her. I wanted to take her home with me, for her to be in my life forever. It was as though she knew me from somewhere else. I wanted to keep her safe forever and ever.

We could communicate, like two adults. I connected completely with her soul. She told me not to worry about her, that she was on earth to teach many souls, many lessons.

I was humbled. I felt I had learned nothing all my life. All of my knowledge from a life lived seemed useless at that point. This baby knew more than I. We're so backward with regard to spiritual things. We really are living in the dark, knowing so little about what matters.

I told her that I loved her and I would think about her every day of my life. That I would send out a little wish, just for her, every day. She beamed back at me.

The time came for Anna to go. It seemed like we'd

been together for an eternity. When she was taken away, I felt empty. But I knew we were connected and I know I'll see her again.

+ + +

That night as I sat in the beautiful gardens of my hotel, my heart opened wider than it ever had before and I cried and cried. My heart had been touched by an angel, an angel in this physical world. Anna had opened my heart in a way that changed me forever. I have never been the same since. That a tiny baby could do that to me is a great miracle. She taught me that every single soul on the earth needs love. I'm trying to live that way since, to open my heart to everyone. It's not always easy but when I'm struggling or I'm feeling annoyed or put out by someone, I'll see Anna's face in front of me. To date, she has affected me more than any other human being in my life.

Every day I send a little wish and a message to her soul. And I do my best to live up to her message.

# THIRTEEN

## THE NECKLACE: SPARKLING GEMS AND HEAVY ROCKS

Each of us has what I like to call a Necklace. It's made up of the people in our life and we wear it every day. It can't be taken off. Our necklace makes us who we are. Some stones weigh us down; some illuminate our faces, lighten our being – like my Anna. All of our gems and their links are stepping stones to others, to new experiences, to new people. We should try not to close ourselves off to the possibility of meeting new people. We can never know how they will influence or help us, or we them. Everyone who touches our life is a different stone on our individual necklace.

My father was, and is, the rarest diamond that I have had the privilege to wear. This stone provides me with a love and security that carries me through the hard times. He is the brightest shining diamond and I hope some of his qualities have rubbed off on me.

My mother was the heaviest rock. We clashed a lot but I see now that this stone challenged me to do better and to grow to be my own person without always needing the approval of others. Three years before she passed over, my relationship with my mother started to change. We came to know each other better. I chiselled away at this heavy stone and found a rare jewel hidden within it. I realised that she had had her own struggles and that her strength was the wonderful legacy she left me.

I have three brothers and nine sisters; twelve different-coloured stones. Their colours have alternately sparkled and dulled, at different times in my life and in our relationships. Each of these individual stones – among them, a ruby, a pearl, a sapphire – brings depth to my necklace. And if I lost any of them, my necklace would lose an element of its sparkle.

Dazzling and bright, my three children enhanced my necklace. They needed polishing, protecting and tending to every day and, since their arrival, I guard my necklace with all my might.

My four grandchildren found their way onto my necklace: Molly, Tate, Patrick and Tessa. These precious little charms are the most joyful and light of all. They came at a time when my necklace needed reviving with innocence, laughter and new energy.

I have other gems – friends and people I have encountered, people in this book – that will stay around my neck for my lifetime. Others sat there briefly, and then the link became weak and they fell away when I wasn't looking. Of course, we all encounter heavy rocks, and sometimes these can be so powerful as to influence other people in our life, other relationships, and to steal their shine. When these rocks of little value become so cumbersome as to weigh us down, they must be removed and put away with good wishes and blessings.

Each of us has a necklace with a story to tell; a thing of history, a thing of beauty. The links are our teachers, neighbours and colleagues who hold the stones firmly, threading the stages of our lives together. In the next part of this final chapter, some of my links and stones recall our meeting and how I then became part of the necklace they wear.

## Recollections and Testimonies

*In the earliest days, when my mother was only beginning to realise she had some kind of ability, Emma, a new friend of mine whom mum had never met, phoned one evening to talk to me. Mum was washing the dishes in the kitchen, but could hear my side of the conversation in the adjoining sitting room.*

*Out of nowhere, mum started firing questions at me.*

*"Ask Emma does she know Kate."*

*I knew myself that Emma had a close friend called Kate but I passed on the question.*

*"Yeah, I've a good friend called Kate," was Emma's puzzled reply.*

"Ask her if she's always laughing. I can see a big wide smile."

I did as I was told.

"Yes, actually, she does."

"Emma was looking in a window today, looking at jewellery. But she didn't buy anything," said mum.

I relayed this.

Emma stayed silent for a minute. Then: "Yes. I was looking at rings in a jeweller's window with my boyfriend this afternoon. We didn't go in. We just looked in the window."

None of us knew what was happening. Least of all mum. She was wondering where the information was coming from. She was just doing the dishes in the kitchen. She wasn't meditating, trying to home in, nothing. And she didn't know Emma at all. She asked aloud, 'Who is speaking? Where is this information coming from?' She heard the name Daniel.

"Does Emma know Daniel? He has passed over."

Again, I was the go-between. Mum still with her back to me, busy at the sink.

"He's my cousin. He died very young. He lived in England."

I held the receiver up so Emma could hear mum as she described the apartment block where he lived, the circumstances surrounding his death, and the name of the person who had helped him. He wanted Emma to know that he was more at peace now that he had had this chance to speak with her. Could she please let the family know that he was doing well, that he was happy.

*We were all astounded. Emma couldn't believe her ears, but she verified that everything was true.*

*Mum wasn't finished, but now there was a new line of questioning: "Who cycles a lot? Who was in a cycling club?"*

*Emma squealed. "It's my parents. My parents cycle a lot. They met in a cycling club."*

*Wiping down the worktops now. "Ask her who is known as Dolier?"*

*I put the question to Emma.*

*"Ah, come on! That's just too much. An old friend of mine – we all know him as Dolier – came in to see me today at work. I hadn't seen him in years."*

*Emma and I still talk about that phone call. It was an amazing evening. My mother had never met her or spoken to her. She was just working away at the sink and being flooded with information from an opportunist spirit! This call showed that if spirits want to communicate, they will; they'll find an instrument to do it and they'll get their message through. Since then, mum has been an instrument that the spirits use to pass messages to their loved ones, to heal them.*

*A medium in rubber gloves.*

Shauna Brazil

+ + +

*It was 23 years since my dad passed over and hardly a day went by when I didn't think of him. I constantly asked myself if there was something for us to look* forward to when we left this world. Perhaps another life? After much consideration, I finally decided to make an appointment with a well-known and highly regarded medium, Margaret Brazil. It was May 2001, a beautiful summer day.

Feeling very nervous, I made my way to Margaret's house, not knowing what to expect. Margaret opened the door, smiled, and welcomed me in. I knew straight away that I had made the right decision.

"Who is Matthew?" Margaret asked as I walked into her hall.

"Oh my God! Matthew's my dad."

"Well, he's here. He's been here for the last twenty minutes, waiting for you."

"Thank God I'm not late!"

We sat and the reading began.

"Your dad is telling me that he died of lung cancer. He tells me he had a big operation, but it was too late. He remembers the days and hours before he passed over very clearly."

Margaret gave me the names of the family members and friends who were around his bed at the time that he passed.

"Who is Mary?"

"That's my mum."

"Matthew asks that you keep an eye on her. He knows you are very good to her but he says her legs are very bad and she's going to have a lot of falls."

This was very true. Mum actually died as a result of a bad fall some years later.

*"Your brother Paul's birthday is about now."*

*"It is."*

Dad also gave Margaret the names of seven or eight friends who were particularly good to him during his illness.

*"You've moved house recently. You're out in the country now, in a little village that he knows. He remembers having a drink in the pub there once. He says the trees and shrubs around the house are beautiful. He particularly likes a dark red shrub in the corner of the back garden."*

I was blown away when Margaret said, *"He wants to know what the story is with his dining room table. He's saying it's a right mess."*

Dad was right. It was a right mess. His dining room table was in my house now and covered in CDs and other things I had been working on. I had run out the door that morning without clearing it away and cleaning it, the way I usually would.

*"Your dad is giving me the name William – known as Billy. He says they are together now."*

*"He's my cousin. He passed over the same year as my dad. He was only 21. Dad thought the world of him."*

Dad went on to describe his own father, whom I remembered very well. He said that he was *"game ball"*.

This was amazing, because that was the expression that my grandfather always used. If anyone asked him how he was feeling, he'd always say, *"I'm game ball."*

*Dad talked about his two brothers and sister-in-law, Anne, who had recently passed over. "Anne is watching over Thomas."*

*Thomas was her son, who had lost his sight a couple of years earlier.*

*"Anne asks that you let Thomas know that she is very happy, and out of all her pain and suffering."*

*"Can you please ask my dad if he knows I had a baby after he passed on?"*

*"Yes, a beautiful little girl. He is showing me her pink garments. Who was it got flowers three days ago?"*

*I guessed it was my daughter, Elaine. Her birthday had been three days before, May 18th.*

*"Your dad says they're in her hall on a 'big ugly table' and are a 'funny-looking colour'."*

*I went to visit Elaine that evening and couldn't believe my eyes. There, inside her hall door, on a very large table, were a bunch of peculiarly coloured peachy roses.*

Geraldine McGann

+ + +

*My brother Paul had passed away a short time before. I was very sceptical about mediums. In my mind, there was no way that a person would be able to speak with the dead. Just no way. Once you're dead, you're dead. But my sister Dinah had been in touch with Margaret to arrange a reading and she asked me to drive her. I* said I would, but there was no way I was going in myself. Dinah came out teary-eyed and smiling. She was very impressed, which surprised me.

Without thinking, and with a bit of encouragement from my sister, I went in. Margaret immediately said that Des – a work colleague and a very good friend of mine – was there. There was no delay or lead in. I said hello, sat down, and there was Des, full of chat and personality. Margaret gave me very accurate information about Des; things that Dinah wouldn't even have known. He was very honest about his life, his marriage. He also told me not to be upset about not making it to the funeral. He understood why it was impossible for me to be there. I got great comfort from this as I had carried a lot of guilt about this. He had passed away only six weeks previously. I was totally taken aback.

The reading went on. The next spirit to come through was my brother Paul. He gave lots of very accurate information about our times together, our family circumstances, how he had passed. Until that point, I had no closure – the family had no closure – on how or why exactly he had died. Margaret described accurately the symptoms, the physical signs, his very last moments, and the underlying causes of his death. There was no way in this world that Margaret could have known any of this.

I became a believer in so many things that day. There was no doubt in my mind that this was all true; that my brother and my friend were there in that room.

*At this stage, my sister Maureen was still alive. Paul described her, our sister, and where she lived. Paul told me that she was going through a very difficult time with her health and her marriage. I was not aware of this at the time. I hoped that he was wrong, but I knew deep inside that what he was saying – what Margaret was saying – was the truth. Paul spoke to me about Maureen's illness and the events that would lead up to her death. I feel that I came to terms with Maureen's deteriorating health over the next year much better as a result of this reading. I was able to be there for her in a more calm and accepting way. I knew she would be leaving this life to go back to Paul, who would look after her.*

*I decided to make contact with Margaret myself for a reading after Maureen died. Paul had described her illness and its developing stages to me. I watched her go through everything that he had told me would happen. And then, one year to the day – on his first anniversary – Maureen joined him in the next life.*

*I went to see Margaret shortly after Maureen died. I didn't say why I was there. Maureen came through immediately. I was shocked because she had passed on so recently. She described, in detail, what had happened to her and how she had died. She had cirrhosis of the liver. She talked about the symptoms of her illness, how her immune system had broken down. She described the morning when she left her house to pick up a newspaper at the shop and collapsed at the gate. Her death was the result of a massive heart attack that morning.*

*She spoke about her funeral and her son and daughter. She asked that I would be there for the children should they need me. I felt like I was speaking to Maureen at the time, not to Margaret. I felt great comfort.*

*John, my baby brother, passed on a year later. So, for three years in a row, in the same month, I had lost a sibling. I made an appointment to see Margaret for the third time. She didn't know that I had been bereaved again.*

*I walked in and she said, "I have Paul, Maureen and John here." Those were her exact words. And then: "John is younger. He is the youngest." John's death was very difficult to take. I had recently learned that he had developed a drug addiction. None of the family had been aware of this during his life. That day, he spoke to me for the first time about his addiction and how it grew, and how he had developed hepatitis. He spoke then of his treatment, his hospitalisation, how his breath became very short and how, at the end, he was only able to communicate with his eyes. This was all absolutely true. He talked about us sitting at his side for his final three weeks, none of us understanding entirely what was going on. He showed Margaret his nails – discoloured, a dark black colour. She could see his emaciated face, his eyes sunken in his head. He said he was embarrassed at us seeing him this way. He said he regretted many things in his life, his drug use and his finding comfort in it. Nobody in the family had ever known. He told me he was happy and at peace now, "in full health and in full spirit". He was with Paul and Maureen.*

*Before I met Margaret I had been very sceptical about clairvoyants and mediums and spirituality. Since the day I first met her, I am a true believer. She has an inspiring gift and has given me great faith and great peace in my life. Today is Maureen and Paul's anniversary.*

Larry Hennessy
Dublin, 2008

+ + +

*Margaret said that my mum and dad had come through to speak to me. She experienced quite severe chest pain and said that both of them had had heart problems. This was correct. She described my dad perfectly, right down to the way he dressed. She said he was a headmaster in a school. He was. She mentioned that I had four children, one named Pauric. She said my parents wanted to talk about him. I had just made a major decision to allow him to leave school but was fighting with myself over it. We were brought up to believe you stayed at school, no matter what. My dad came through and said that the decision I had made about Pauric was the right one and that my son would thank me for it later. He said that I was right to break with tradition and that what was right for us as kids was not necessarily right for my kids. This was a great relief for me.*

My mother was pleased that Pauric was attending St James's Hospital and finally having his operation. Margaret said she was laughing while she was saying this. I smiled. When he was very young, my mother had asked me to take him to an orthodontist, as she thought he had a problem with his teeth. I disagreed, but it turned out that she was right and needed a procedure done. We were waiting for the date at this point.

Margaret said that my other son Chris had been badly affected by my marriage break-up but was not very good at talking about his feelings. This was very true. My dad said that Chris was sulky and not to let him away with it. This was very typical of something he would've said when he was alive.

Margaret kept breaking into Irish. She said this was my father speaking. He was fluent in Irish but could never manage to teach me. I think he was poking fun at me! Margaret said she could sense that he was very funny and outspoken, while my mother was quite reserved. This was spot on.

My parents said that someone I worked with was pushing all the wrong buttons with me but to stick with it as this person wasn't right for the job and wouldn't last long. Very soon after, this turned out to be the case.

Margaret said she could see a house – it was open and full of light, in the process of being built. It was closer to where I had originally come from and very close to my mother's heart. My mother said she was *"glad to be back". We were building in my mother's home town in Cavan.*

*Margaret said that my dad knew I could sense his presence sometimes. This was true, but I didn't tell Margaret when or where. I didn't need to. She said "it is in the car in the morning on the way to work". I couldn't believe it. This was exactly the case. He said he enjoyed our time together on our own. She then said that the baby I had lost some years before sometimes travelled with us, as he was often with his granddad.*

Maura, 2004

**+ + +**

*Meeting Margaret was one of the most important days of my life. This woman changed my vision of life in an amazing way. There are so many things she has done for me and my family that we will be eternally grateful to her. Through her spiritual healing, she has made miracles happen in my life. There have been so many moments where I saw no light. She helped me to see the light, to understand situations better and deal with them in the best way we can.*

*I don't live near Margaret, I never have. I don't even live in Ireland. Yet her healing gift and her reading have no limitations. No time differences stop her from healing. What I most like about her is that she is humble about it all.*

*Some years ago, I was living in Paris. I received a call from my father, who lives in Colombia, South*

America. It was one o'clock in the afternoon in Paris, seven in the morning in Colombia. My father has heart problems. He wasn't feeling well and told me the cardiologist had scheduled a procedure. He was very worried and asked if I could please call Margaret. I did. It was twelve noon in Ireland. I told Margaret I had my dad on the other line. I didn't have to say anything else.

Right away, she was transported to my parents' home in Colombia. She saw my dad having breakfast. She described to me in great detail what he was wearing, the dining room where he sat, what he was eating; brown toast with boiled eggs. Everything she described was true. She had never been in Colombia, to this house.

She could see from where she stood in the kitchen that he wasn't really alone at that big dining table. Sitting around the table, keeping him company, were his parents and a close friend of his who had passed away recently.

Everything was happening very fast, for they had a lot to say to my father; they would tell Margaret, she would tell me and I would tell my dad. My grandmother, who passed away in 1971, was the first one to send a message for my dad. Her name is Olive. She said many comforting things to my dad and then Margaret – Olive – broke into song on the end of the phone. She sang a song called "Cool Spanish Eyes". I didn't know the song but I repeated the words as Margaret sung them to my dad on the other phone. I

*had never heard it before, but my father started to cry.*
*This was their song! His mother used to sing it to him*
*when he was a little boy to make him feel better.*
*Amazing. My grandparents and his friend talked in*
*detail about the operation that my father would have*
*and told him exactly what would happen – down to*
*the number of stents that would be put in – and that it*
*would be very successful.*

*Needless to say, my father was extremely grateful to*
*the spirits and of course to Margaret. I was in complete*
*awe, to know that life is much more than what can be*
*seen. This knowledge brings very deep healing with it.*
*My father is still well and cares very deeply for*
*Margaret.*

Martha de Lima
Milan

✚ ✚ ✚

*I have had the pleasure of being read by Margaret not*
*once, but twice. She was shockingly accurate in the*
*details that she gave me from my loved ones. She was*
*able to describe family members and friends, both*
*living and dead, in amazing detail, getting their*
*personalities and their humour down to a tee.*

*Each time Margaret would tell me things that no-*
*one could possibly know about the person, except for*
*myself. Or she would mention an incident that only I*
*would have known about. This experience was*
*upsetting, but also a great comfort. I was able to have*

*some unanswered questions answered, which sent shivers down my spine.*

*Margaret creates a wonderfully warm and calm environment as soon as you sit down, and I would recommend her without hesitation for anyone who would like a reading.*

Wendy Baum

October 2004

**+ + +**

*I first met Margaret in September 1996. My mum and dad were not long dead and I was curious about the possibility of seeing them, but I didn't have any real belief in the afterlife. Margaret was not what I was expecting at all. She was tall and blonde, and had a warm smile. She told me that my dad wanted to say sorry for any wrong he had done me. He wanted me to believe it was him so he showed Margaret that his shirt was undone and he was having difficulty breathing. My dad never did up his shirt because it made him feel like he couldn't breathe. She told me the songs he sang for us as kids and asked her to tell my girls Amy and Hollie that he loved them.*

*Then my mum was there. Margaret told me my mum had died of cancer and she thanked me for nursing her. She thanked me for the yellow roses I put in with her just after she passed on. No-one knew this; only me.*

*My reading lasted two hours and moved me to tears.*

*She not only told me about my past, but also my present and my future. Margaret began to move her hand along my arm and over the top half of my body. Her hand never touched me but the heat was unreal. She told me I had had surgery to my lungs and my chest. I had had lung surgery twice.*

*If I were to write down all the things that she told me, everything that she knew about my family, my very private fears and worries, my job – I would be here all day. This lady gave me peace, hope, healing and a solid belief in a life after this. I have sent many friends and they have all been amazed by what they are told. I hope Margaret keeps up her work because she is truly gifted.*

Janet

1999

**✝ ✝ ✝**

*My first reading with Margaret was in April 1996. She gave me a very detailed description of the house I moved to when I was twelve years old. I was only visiting Margaret's house when she lapsed into this. She described standing at the gate, then walking up the gravel drive, going up steps, turning left and going into a porch with geranium plants. As she entered the house, she picked up feelings of loneliness, isolation, darkness, no positivity, no home fires, no baking. She saw a man wearing glasses and an Aran cardigan with wooden buttons coming toward her. She could feel his emotions; his loneliness, feeling like he gave in all of* the time, that he just existed. That he had no control over his situation. This was my father. Margaret told me he went grey very early. He had no fight in him. I was amazed that she could be so accurate.

Margaret then went up the stairs and saw a bedroom to the left where a lovely lady spent a lot of time alone. She was surrounded by beautiful, feminine things. She was very glamorous and stylish, but also very aloof. She felt she couldn't cope with what was going on below. She seemed very severe. She criticised her husband so much that he had lost any self-respect that he ever had. I was stunned as this was a very accurate description of my mother.

Margaret then went up another flight of stairs and saw a young man with glasses and books under his arm. He seemed very studious. This was my brother. As she descended the staircase, Margaret saw a young girl wearing a beautiful white dress with her hair tied back in a bow. She was standing behind her father, which she did a lot. Not wanting to go upstairs, Margaret said this girl was a bit of a tomboy and as a young girl had nobody to play with. I was absolutely stunned. I remembered the dress. It was one of the only dresses I wore as a child and I hated it. I was a tomboy and I had felt very isolated and lonely growing up.

As I had only buried my mother that year and was coming to terms with her death and my relationship with her, this experience was a real eye-opener. I went home puzzled as to how Margaret could have seen all this as she knew nothing of me or my childhood and I *would never have talked about my parents or that house to anyone.*

Carolyn

**✝ ✝ ✝**

*My first meeting with Margaret was in the sitting room in her house. It was 1997. It left me feeling amazed and unable to explain how she could tell me about my daughters, parents, sister and other relations who had passed on. It was the first time I had experienced anything like it.*

*When Margaret entered the room, she looked beautiful. There was a golden aura all about her. I felt very relaxed. The background music tape kept getting louder and louder, and she explained to me about spirits and their energy.*

*My deceased sister spoke to me through Margaret and answered a question that I put to her. I was amazed. When she was alive, my sister had an unusual expression she used quite often, and Margaret said it to me twice.*

*I was 72 years old at the time, so many people who were important to me had passed away – and they were all in Margaret's room that day. She held my hand and told me that they are only ever a call away.*

*I left her room without any doubt that she is right. I still feel it all around me. I thank Margaret from the bottom of my heart for her help and wish her health and happiness.*

Deborah Kenna

+ + +

*Meeting Margaret changed my spiritual life completely. I have always had faith in God but until I met her, I didn't realise how close He is to us, how much He really loves us. Many spiritual doors have opened for me since I encountered Margaret in 1997. She is one of the most natural, down-to-earth people I have ever met, yet she is the most spiritual person I know. She understands so much of this life and also of the other side that, without even realising, she helps you so much.*

*It is through Margaret that I realised that loved ones who have passed away are still near us, helping us, still love us. With her wonderful gift, she has held my hand and shown me that new world where spirits' biggest purpose is to help us grow spiritually and learn to heal ourselves. That is what makes Margaret a great healer. She wants people to heal themselves. She doesn't consider herself a Guide, just a channel. She is guided by a spirit, who only does what is best for you. She will not work for you, she shows you how to do it yourself, to walk your own path in life.*

*I didn't know what to expect before I spoke to her. I was told she was a medium and a healer. My grandmother, who died in 1971, came in immediately, giving me lots of evidence and advice. Just knowing that they aren't really "dead" is amazing.*

*Margaret has since given me healing. Words cannot*

*express how wonderful she is. The benefits are both physical and spiritual. I had a very severe lower back pain. Even though I had been to doctors and osteopaths, it would not cease. I was desperate, so I decided to phone Margaret. She sent me healing every day for a month. I have no pain anymore.*

*Margaret travels with her mind. All of this has been done over the phone. I live in Paris.*

Madeleine
2006

✛ ✛ ✛

*When I first went to meet Margaret, I didn't know what to expect. I had never been to a medium in my life. Before I had closed the door in her house, she asked me if I knew anyone else by the name of Margaret. This was my mother's name.*

*Margaret told me that my mother was very excited that I was there. She was glad I was doing some courses and said that I would make a very good counsellor. She said my mother was talking very fast, as she was excited to have the opportunity to do so. She said that James was there too; trying to get through and speak but because my mother was speaking so fast, he was finding it difficult. This was my dad.*

*Margaret asked who Frank was. As she asked, she put her hand over her chest. Frank had died of a heart attack. Then she talked about Brendan, while putting her hand on her head. She said that Brendan had had a very violent death, with head injuries. She said my dad had been with him in the ambulance before the rest of us got there.*

*My mother popped in again to say that life was like knitting – one stitch at a time. My dad mentioned how much I loved lilies, which made me smile. Margaret was very sensitive and gentle throughout. I found the whole experience a great comfort and I felt reassured and safe with her. When I left I felt extremely happy.*

Phyllis

1998

+ + +

*My teenage son asked me if he could change bedrooms. There was banging at night-time and he couldn't sleep. I had felt a presence around me, heard the noises too. It had been going on for weeks. The house was very cold all the time, whether the heat was on or not. Intense, icy cold. I could smell smoke in my bedroom, loud banging along the radiator beside my bed that would go on and on; the washing machine was being turned off mid-cycle; all kinds of things were happening in the house. My son started hearing his name being called and feeling the weight of a hand on him. One morning, I woke up and couldn't get out of the bed. I physically couldn't move. I was being held. There was a force on my legs that was pinning me down. It frightened the life out of me. I rang my husband John. I was hysterical, so much so that he left work and came home.*

*The priest came around later that day. I'll never forget it. He walked into the sitting room.*

*"Frances, you look very distressed."*

*"So would you be. There's spirits all over the house."*

*He looked sceptical.*

*"There ARE. I am living here. Living with them."*

*He blessed every corner of the house, but unfortunately it had little effect.*

*I started waking up in the middle of the night to these presences in the room. I tried to get through to Gerry Ryan. I got all kinds of suggestions from everybody, from putting lavender in the house to sprinkling holy water. I did everything. I was looking over my shoulder all of the time. Wondering if they were watching me getting dressed. I started to get anxious and depressed. I went to the doctor.*

*After several nights in a row waking up at three in the morning, I couldn't stick it anymore. I got up, dressed myself and walked down the road to hail a taxi. I went to my mother's house and got into bed. But it made no difference. The spirits came. It was me they were following, me they wanted to talk to.*

*I was sick with fear. It doesn't frighten me when it happens now, though.*

*I contacted Margaret. My sister and I had been to her some time before. I was ready to try anything. She came to my house and tuned in to them straight away. She told me there was a baby in my room – she had passed on in a fire – and there was an alcoholic man in my son's room. I didn't know whether I believed her or* not; to be honest, I didn't care. I didn't need an explanation. I just wanted it all to stop; I wanted whatever or whoever it was to get out of my house.

We all left the house and Margaret in it. When I came back into the house; it was warm. Warm like it had never been. She told me about three spirits she had found. The next day, I found a half a string of strange rosary beads on the floor in the bedroom and the other half in my car.

Margaret explained that I was a lighthouse for spirits. They could see me brightly, and they were latching on to me to help them pass over. I suppose it made sense, in a way, but still – I just wanted my house back. And I got it. The house was peaceful again, for a time. But it was only the beginning. To this day, lost and frightened spirits still find me but now I can help them myself. Margaret helped me to unlock my own gift and I'm very grateful to her for that.

Frances
June 2008

+ + +

## Symbols

I am fully united and integrated with the spirits when they come through and they are always very clear in their messages. They converse fully with me in conversation, just as the sitter in front of me can. The majority of spirits can communicate with me as they did when they lived; they can sing and chat and dance – whatever they feel is needed for the sitter to believe in them.

There are occasions, however, when I encounter spirits who find it more difficult than others to articulate their messages, to speak clearly or to be heard fully. When I encounter a slow or difficult spirit, I must be very patient and gentle as they try to impart their messages to their loved ones. We are all different. No two people are alike, so no two spirits are alike.

In these cases, spirits may support their message, the reading, with symbols so that I can understand them more clearly and communicate more fully on their behalf.

Every medium has different symbols – indeed, I understand that some mediums only "speak" in symbols – images that mean different things and express very particular messages that are easily deciphered by them.

In the early days, I learned what the different symbols meant, what the spirits were trying to convey to me in showing them. They used personal memories and associations of mine to teach me. Over the years, I have built up a very extensive repertoire of symbols.

For example, I associate Christchurch in Dublin with New Year's Eve. So when the spirits show me Christchurch and throngs of people around the area, I have come to know that New Year's Eve is always the message. A lady sat with me one afternoon twenty years ago, when I was learning my symbols. Her mother came through. Immediately, I was shown a busy Christchurch and I knew instinctively what this meant.

"Your mother is here. She is showing me New Year's Eve."

"Yes. She died that day – December 31st."

And so it remains. For the spirits, for me, Christchurch always denotes New Year's Eve.

The symbol for cancer, for me, is closed eyes. I don't know why this has come to be – there are easier ways of showing disease – but, in recent years, as soon as I see a pair of closed eyes I know that this is how the spirit passed on. This is how they communicate their cancer to me.

Some symbols are very straightforward. A blackboard and chalk is my symbol for teaching. This is a clear image; I know immediately that I can say with confidence that the person was a teacher in this life. Another simple symbol is the image of a plane with a plaster on it. I know then that the person was in a plane crash. Thankfully, I have only seen this a handful of times over the years. It's very startling when it comes into view. And it's always accurate. I never see it unless the spirit passed over as a result of a plane crash. Likewise, the simple image of two crossed swords always denotes conflict.

I learned early on that the vision of a small flame means somebody passed over in a fire. Just a flame, as though from a candle. No clouds of smoke, no raging heat. Just a small, clear flame. Again, it has always been right.

When a spirit wants to impress upon me the existence of "twins", I will hear the following song playing in my head:

*"Twenty tiny fingers, twenty tiny toes,*
*Two angel faces, each with a turned-up nose*
*One looks like mummy, with a cute little curl on top*
*And the other one's got a big bald spot*
*Exactly like his pop"*

I've actually never heard this song any other time, and it's not a song I knew previously, but when I hear it in my mind, I know the message is twins. It's always been my sign for twins. I knew immediately what it was the first time I heard it a long time ago. Why they didn't just say "twins" or show me a pair of similar-looking babies, or something, I just don't know!

Another symbol that comes up quite regularly is what looks like a child's drawing of a half-moon filled with a lot of black, pencil-coloured shading. This is my symbol for depression. In accordance with how severe and debilitating the depression is, it will be darker and thicker or coloured with lighter pencil-gray strokes.

+ + +

You don't have to see symbols or go to a medium to know that your loved ones live on. You don't have to "see" their spirits to know they exist. Sometimes, if a spirit is close to you, lights may flicker; a warm feeling may touch you – as if one side of your body is next to a warm fire; they will pop into your mind like photos;

you will meet them in your dreams; you might find a lost object or come across a forgotten, shared place; your little child might stare at one place in a room; or your hair might feel as though it's being gently touched.

Spirits do give us many signs to get our attention, but we let them go unnoticed as our minds may be too logical or too busy to make them out. Just as it can be hard to find a person in a very crowded and packed railway station, we know they are there but with so much else going on in the station, we can't identify them, can't find them.

You won't feel your loved ones closer in the place where they are buried or in the room where they died, because they are free. They come to us on the energy of love and kindness. This bond can never be severed or broken and does not attach to only one place. They are still there for us, as they were when they were alive and on this earth. They just don't have a physical body that we can see. But they have their minds, their personalities. They still listen, they still understand. You can still share your life and your concerns with them. They are always within earshot.

Try to attribute what you might dismiss as coincidences to the spirit world and to acknowledge them. Say thank you, in your mind. Just like when they lived, they feel wonderful when they are noticed or appreciated.

*Even greater miracles than these,*
*Ye shall do also.*

Jesus

*To Steve, Shauna and Glen,*

Had I never known you; what a loss!

You awoke in me something so strong, so powerful, so unfamiliar that it took my breath away and left me speechless.

This tiny creature so quiet and so frail had the capacity to change everything about me. My perception of who I really was and the world as I had seen it. I thought you were completely unaware, sleeping there, but now I know that you knew more than I.

I was in awe of you and knew that you would teach me my greatest lessons.

You guided me to have patience, courage and loyalty. You taught me to trust myself, because you trusted me so completely. You taught me the pleasure of the simple things – gifts of giving and sharing. You guided me to be patient and to see the good in other people, as you did.

You loved me unconditionally whether I was fat, thin, ugly, small, tall, blonde, brunette, rich or poor. Because of your love, I grew in confidence.

In my dark moods, you cherished me and seemed to sense my inner thoughts.

Every day brought new treasures and pleasures. The satisfaction and sense of achievement I felt when you were fed, warm and happy. A beautiful smile first thing in the morning and last thing at night.

You taught me to lighten up a little, to just let you grow.

Over time, you gently prised my fingers from your arms and I came to realise that I had to let you be. You are your own person and I am mine.

Out of all of this, I think I got the better deal.

I must ask you one day and find out how you feel.

I could fill pages with words but never enough to express the joy, wonder and learning that came from a tiny seed.

**Margaret Brazil**
**September 1995**